A Curriculum Guide for Leaders

A Curriculum Guide for Middle Leaders is a comprehensive guide to the curriculum for middle leaders and subject leaders. Designed to support middle leaders in both primary and secondary schools, it explores every aspect of successful curriculum leadership beginning with intent and moving on to cover implementation and impact. It is closely aligned to the new inspection framework, and demystifies key terminology including selection, sequencing, progression, and interleaving.

Written in an accessible Q&A format, the book equips readers with the tools and knowledge they need to construct an imaginative and effective subject curriculum, and prepares them to successfully take part in 'deep dives'. There are also templates and practical tools drawn from sources of good practice across the country that can be easily adapted for individual subjects and schools.

Addressing the key concerns of both experienced leaders and those new to the role, this essential resource encourages readers to think deeply about the curriculum and how it is taught, enabling them to make a significant contribution to whole school improvement.

Richard Steward is an educational consultant with extensive experience as a teacher and headteacher. He has taught in a variety of schools in a thirty-year career and has worked as a part-time lecturer with The Open University. He has worked with the National College for Teaching and Learning and been involved in a wide range of national educational research projects. His previous books include *The Gradual Art of School Improvement* and *The Toxic Classroom*.

A Curriculum Guide for Middle Leaders

Intent, Implementation and Impact in Practice

Richard Steward

Routledge
Taylor & Francis Group

LONDON AND NEW YORK

First published 2021
by Routledge
2 Park Square, Milton Park, Abingdon, Oxon OX14 4RN

and by Routledge
52 Vanderbilt Avenue, New York, NY 10017

Routledge is an imprint of the Taylor & Francis Group, an informa business

British Library Cataloguing-in-Publication Data
A catalogue record for this book is available from the British Library

Library of Congress Cataloging-in-Publication Data

Names: Steward, Richard, 1961- author.
Title: A curriculum guide for middle leaders : intent, implementation, and impact in practice / Richard Steward.
Identifiers: LCCN 2020038791 | ISBN 9780367610968 (hardback) | ISBN 9780367610982 (paperback) | ISBN 9781003104100 (ebook)
Subjects: LCSH: Curriculum planning. | Educational leadership.
Classification: LCC LB2806.15 .S75 2101 | DDC 375/.001--dc23
LC record available at https://lccn.loc.gov/2020038791

ISBN: 978-0-367-61096-8 (hbk)
ISBN: 978-0-367-61098-2 (pbk)
ISBN: 978-1-003-10410-0 (ebk)

Typeset in Melior
by SPi Global, India

Contents

APPENDICES   167

Introduction

Middle leadership in context

School leadership is a relatively new concept. The use of the term did not become commonplace until the end of the last century but since then it has come to be regarded as fundamental to the development of successful schooling. The initial focus was on headteachers and principals, and, for a time, the cult of the 'hero head' dominated educational discourse. It quickly became clear, however, that headteachers were not the only leaders in schools. The role of senior leaders began to attract the attention of educational researchers, a shift which inevitably led to an understanding of the vital role played by middle leaders. School leadership began to be acknowledged as collegiate, with leaders at every level. Indeed, the teacher in the classroom is a leader of learning, guiding the education of thirty or so pupils every day.

Middle leadership is now firmly under the spotlight thanks, in part, to the introduction of Ofsted's 2019 Education Inspection Framework (EIF) which places heads of department and subject leaders at the heart of the inspection process. This has resulted in a sea change in the way middle leaders are regarded in schools, although it is perhaps fair to say that the revised framework is merely responding to the changing nature of the middle leadership role. Ofsted has simply recognised the importance of middle leaders in shaping and delivering teaching and learning in schools.

The term 'middle leader' covers an increasingly wide range of roles including key stage leader, curriculum area leader, pastoral/year team leader, subject leader, special educational needs coordinator (SENCO) and head of department. Nor should we overlook the middle leaders in the administration teams who play an important part in running schools, especially in multi-academy trusts where office managers and finance assistants may not be members of the senior leadership team but nevertheless carry out key management functions. There are also middle leaders who may move between schools: specialist leaders of education (SLEs), for example. The majority of middle leaders manage a team or, like SLEs, exert significant influence over groups of people. They also have considerable influence over matters such as pedagogy, curriculum planning, appraisal, and quality assurance, and it is here that their role has expanded significantly in recent years.

The introduction of the EIF has led to greater recognition by headteachers and governors of the increasing complexity of the role of the middle leaders in their schools. It is clear that the intense scrutiny of the new inspection framework has led to a real sense of increased responsibility and the new focus on the curriculum has served to highlight just how important subject and curriculum leaders are to the success of the school. Senior leaders may be responsible for the overarching vision, but it is heads of department and subject leaders who are directly responsible for curriculum content and classroom pedagogy. The EIF has therefore had a positive impact in that it has highlighted the important role middle leaders play in schools but, in doing so, it has left some colleagues – those who have not moved with the times – somewhat exposed. This has meant that schools have been scrambling to ensure that their middle leaders have the necessary curriculum and pedagogical skills to cope with the new framework.

A middle leader post, whether focused on subject or pastoral leadership, is now a sophisticated undertaking. In addition to the increased responsibilities connected with the EIF, middle leaders now need excellent subject knowledge, a good understanding of how the curriculum works, both at subject and at whole school level, and a sophisticated understanding of contemporary pedagogy. They need to understand whole school policy and have the skills to work within its confines, and they need to be able to align their subject or pastoral objectives with the wider aims of the school. This means stronger relationships with senior leaders and governors and, to some extent, greater autonomy, though this is constrained by the need to work with other middle leaders in the context of whole school improvement. Where once upon a time a middle leader was responsible for ordering books and disciplining miscreants, they now perform a much more sophisticated role both in terms of management skills and intellectual engagement. Above all, middle leaders need to be focused on the pupil in the classroom, providing a bridge between the classroom teacher and senior leaders.

The National Professional Qualification for Middle Leadership (NPQML) recognises the complexity of the role.[1] It enables candidates to develop their skills in what it describes as the six key content areas:

1. Strategy and improvement.

2. Teaching and curriculum excellence.

3. Leading with impact.

4. Working in partnership.

5. Managing resources and risks.

6. Increasing capability.

And seven leadership behaviours:

1. Commitment.

2. Collaboration.

3. Personal drive.

4. Resilience.

5. Awareness.

6. Integrity.

7. Respect.

This is a useful summary, but I suspect it will need to be revised in the light of the EIF in order to strengthen the focus on 'curriculum excellence' and to help develop the enhanced relationship between middle and senior leadership.

As long ago as 2003, the National College for School Leadership (NCSL), as it was then called, identified the increasing significance of middle leadership in schools. It undertook what was essentially a literature review which set out to summarise contemporary research in the area. The summary report, titled *The Role and Purpose of Middle Leaders in Schools*, had a significant impact on the profession, identifying both the strengths and weaknesses of middle leaders in schools at the start of the century.[2] Many of its findings are still relevant. It noted that middle leaders played a crucial role in developing and maintaining the nature and quality of pupils' learning experiences, but the ways in which they did this were strongly influenced by the circumstances in which they worked. They recognised the strong rhetoric of collegiality in departments and pastoral teams but also saw that this was sometimes more aspired to than real. In particular, they noted the fact that many middle leaders showed considerable resistance to the idea of monitoring the quality of their colleagues' work in the classroom, something which is still an issue today.

Subject knowledge was seen to provide an important part of professional identity, but this was regarded as something of a barrier, with colleagues reluctant to move beyond their subject specialisms. This was more of a concern in secondary schools where heads of department saw their role as fundamentally subject based whereas primary colleagues were more used to covering broader curriculum areas. The issue in primary schools, however, was concern over subject knowledge itself. A class teacher moving up to a whole school role may well feel equipped to take charge of, say, reading, but science could well be a more exacting challenge.

One of the most interesting findings of the NCSL report was the fact that its authors were unable to find very little research covering the influence of middle leadership on teaching and learning. Nor were they able to find very much at all on the effectiveness of middle leaders' professional development. These findings are still relevant today and will be explored in detail in the pages of this book, but we should also acknowledge that middle leadership has come a long way since 2003. Very few middle leaders regard themselves simply as subject specialists nowadays, though this is still a key part of the role, and there is much greater awareness of its whole school nature. Above all, there is a much greater appreciation of the importance of an understanding of pedagogy, and very few leaders nowadays fail to keep abreast of educational research, whether it is subject based or more general.

The introduction of the EIF has certainly moved things along and will help to address some of the issues identified by the NCSL report. Let us pause for a moment, therefore, and consider what has changed and what Ofsted now expects from middle leaders.

Intent, Implementation, Impact

The new inspection framework focuses on three key areas: intent, implementation and impact. As an outline summary of the role of the middle leader, this is a fairly sensible description and one that I have used to provide the basic structure of this book. It also structures the meetings inspectors have with school leaders during the inspection and the activities undertaken throughout the day.

Inspections begin with detailed discussions about the school's curriculum. The lead inspector will have spent some time on the phone to the headteacher on the day that the inspection is announced with the curriculum as the main agenda item. During that discussion four or five 'deep dives' will have been identified and agreed. The length of the preliminary telephone discussion means that inspectors are able to begin their day by talking to curriculum leaders – those identified during the deep dive discussion. Most of these meetings take place first thing in the morning and therefore kick start the day. Middle leaders now find themselves in the spotlight straightaway. They are therefore key to the inspection process and under much greater scrutiny than ever before.

The Ofsted handbook offers a succinct outline of these initial meetings:

> Inspectors ask about what leaders intend pupils to learn. What are the end points they wish them to reach, what are the key concepts that they need to understand, and in what order will they learn them? They will also ask about pupils' behaviour and attitudes and personal development.[3]

As we shall see, this brief outline paves the way for a wide-ranging and comprehensive discussion. This then leads to a series of lesson visits spread across the first day of the inspection. Curriculum leaders are encouraged to accompany inspectors during lesson visits, enabling them to comment on what they have seen, and it is now good practice for inspectors and middle leaders to look at books together, both in the classroom and as part of a more thorough book scrutiny session:

> Inspectors will visit lessons, talk to individual teachers and pupils, and look at pupils' work (in its widest sense) together with curriculum leaders to see

whether it matches leaders' intentions. Inspectors will then draw all this evidence together from different pupils, classes and year groups.[4]

During the course of an inspection, therefore, middle leaders will find themselves demonstrating many, if not all of the skills which form the core of the NPQML qualification. Their improvement strategies will be central to their account of the curriculum and they will inevitably have to outline their approach to classroom pedagogy. The impact of their leadership will be probed as inspectors evaluate the quality of teaching and learning and begin to draw together the various pieces of evidence gathered during the day. Relationships with colleagues will be key here: inspectors will expect to see a coherent approach to the delivery of the curriculum across the school. This means high level partnership working, shared planning and resource creation, and common goals.

The performance of middle leaders is therefore crucial to the success of an inspection as the grade descriptors for a good judgement make clear:

- Leaders have a clear and ambitious vision for providing high-quality education to all pupils. This is realised through strong, shared values, policies and practice.

- Leaders focus on improving teachers' subject, pedagogical and pedagogical content knowledge in order to enhance the teaching of the curriculum and the appropriate use of assessment. The practice and subject knowledge of staff, including newly qualified teachers, build and improve over time.

- Leaders aim to ensure that all pupils successfully complete their programmes of study. They provide the support for staff to make this possible. They create an inclusive culture and do not allow gaming or off-rolling.

- Leaders engage effectively with pupils and others in their community, including, when relevant, parents, employers and local services. Engagement opportunities are focused and have purpose.

- Leaders engage with their staff and are aware and take account of the main pressures on them. They are realistic and constructive in the way they manage staff, including their workload.[5]

Of course, the middle leadership skills needed to navigate a successful inspection are not new, as both the NCSL summary report and the NPQML demonstrate. The EIF has, however, brought them into much sharper focus. To put it bluntly, there is now no hiding place for weak and complacent middle leaders.

How to use this book

The aim of this book, therefore, is to explore in depth the complexity of the role of today's middle leader, both in primary and secondary settings. It aims not only to provide information and guidance which will be useful in preparing for an inspection but to explore the role of the middle leader *per se*. Whatever inspection framework is put in place, the role of the middle leader will be vital to a school's success and key to improving pupils' education. The EIF is a good starting point but any consideration of leadership needs to go well beyond the pages of the inspection manual. School leadership is about teaching and learning; it is about the success of every pupil in every classroom.

I have adopted a three-part structure mirroring the approach of the EIF: Intent, Implementation and Impact. Each section consists of a series of questions to which answers are supplied. The questions seek to cover the key concerns of middle leaders and are therefore, in essence, a series of curriculum leadership FAQs. Each question is answered as clearly as possible and each one builds upon those that have gone before. The book can therefore be read as a continuous text which seeks to give a comprehensive account of the curriculum leadership role, but it will also be useful to dip into and to use as a reference manual. It is not an academic treatise; it is a practical guide. Key theorists or significant pieces of guidance are referred to occasionally, but the main focus is on the practical application of the curriculum in the classroom. The book concludes with a set of guidance materials drawn from good practice across the country which curriculum leaders may wish to adapt for use in their own schools.

It is hoped that the advice and guidance contained herein will stimulate conversation and encourage further thought. It is by no means a prescriptive account. It may be that, having read it, many of the ideas will be rejected, or completely re-thought, but that's fine. As Gerald Manley Hopkins put it, 'The effect of studying masterpieces is to make me admire and do otherwise'.[6] This book is, admittedly, hardly a masterpiece but Hopkins' injunction to 'do otherwise' may ultimately ensure its usefulness. Curriculum leadership has become a demanding and sophisticated role. The advice and guidance set out here may help to make it seem less daunting and, with luck, more enjoyable.

Notes

1 National Professional Qualification for Middle Leadership (NPQML) (2014). Updated 26 February 2020. https://www.gov.uk/guidance/national-professional-qualification-for-middle-leadership-npqml
2 National College for School Leadership 2003 – Summary Report (2003). A review of literature prepared for NCSL in support of the Leading from the Middle Programme by Nigel Bennett, Wendy Newton, Christine Wise, Philip A Woods and Anastasia Economou of the Centre for Educational Policy and Management. https://dera.ioe.ac.uk/5118/13/download_id=17365&filename=role-purpose-of-middle-leaders-in-schools-summary_Redacted.pdf
3 *School Inspection Handbook*, Handbook for inspecting schools in England under section 5 of the Education Act 2005, (2019) updated September 2019, Reference no: 190017, Crown copyright 2019, p. 26.
4 Ibid. p.26
5 Ibid. p.74.
6 Hopkins, G.M. from a letter in 1888 to Robert Bridges. See *The Letters of Gerard Manley Hopkins to Robert Bridges* (1935) p.291. OUP.

PART

I INTENT

1
What is meant by 'intent'?

'Inspectors ask about what leaders intend pupils to learn.'[1] This somewhat bland statement disguises what is in fact an exceptionally complex topic. A few years ago, a head of department or curriculum leader would have had no hesitation in providing an answer to the question, 'What do you intend your pupils to learn?' The answer was obvious: the material set out in the National Curriculum and the knowledge needed to prepare for national tests. In primary schools, the curriculum is shaped to prepare pupils for the Key Stage 2 tests; in secondary schools, GCSEs and A-Levels provide the direction of travel. In practice, of course, it is not that simple. The increasing importance of national testing, and the accompanying high-stakes accountability culture, encouraged – some might say forced – teachers to focus on examination specifications. However, the inherent commitment and professionalism of teachers has meant that very few focused solely on the demands of the tests. There has always been a great deal of discussion in schools covering almost every aspect of the curriculum. The tests may well provide the end points for both primary and secondary schooling, but the journey to get to those points is a long one.

Teachers have always been able to adapt the National Curriculum programmes of study to suit the needs of their pupils; they have been able to select, emphasise and, sometimes, disregard the suggested skills and topics. They have been able to spend more time on the topics they consider to be of most use and value to pupils, and less on those that seem to have little relevance. They have also been able to bring their own areas of interest and expertise into the classroom, whether by introducing new topics, say, in history or science, or simply by the choice of a new class reader aimed at firing the imagination. Examination syllabuses are obviously more restrictive – pupils need to be well prepared for all the topics likely to occur in the examination papers – but good teachers seek ways to make the material more accessible and more stimulating. Whether this is done by relating topics to contemporary situations, or finding time to insert additional topics, it is clear that in practice, teachers do a great deal more than simply deliver examination specifications.

The introduction of the Education Inspection Framework (EIF) has, however, made discussions of the curriculum much more explicit. Many colleagues will probably not have considered the choices they make regarding their day-to-day teaching as curriculum decisions even though, in effect, that's what they are. A school curriculum is much more than a list of skills and topics, and all good teachers go well beyond National Curriculum programmes of study or examination specifications in their teaching.

The notion of 'intent' is therefore a complex one. It does cover, of course, the intention of delivering the programmes of study and the examination specifications as effectively as possible in order to achieve the best outcomes for pupils, but it also includes a wide range of other curriculum decisions:

- What skills and topics are to be taught?

- When should they be taught?

- In what years?

- At what point in the year?

- At what level should they be taught?

- How long should each topic last?

- In what order should they be taught? How should they be sequenced?

- Does each topic build upon previous topics? How are skills to be steadily developed over the course of a term, year or Key Stage?

- Is each topic to be assessed?

- How is the curriculum content to be differentiated? Should all topics be taught to all pupils or are some more suitable to groups of pupils?

- How does curriculum content relate to ability?

- In planning the curriculum is attention being paid to high ability pupils, those with special educational needs, those with English as an additional language etc?

- Are the planned skills and topics sufficiently challenging?

- What adaptations are to be made to ensure that less able pupils do not fall behind and are able to catch up if they do so?

- How does the curriculum connect with what has gone before or coming next? In other words, does Key Stage 2 prepare pupils for Key Stage 3, and does Key Stage 3 build upon the work done at Key Stage 2. Similarly, does the work planned for Years 10 and 11 prepare pupils not only for GCSEs but for A-Levels too?

- Does the curriculum seek to equip pupils with the cultural capital they need to be able to really benefit from the new learning?

- What extra-curricular opportunities will be available to enhance pupils' understanding of the topics covered?

- What literacy and numeracy skills will need to be covered to enable pupils to cope with the various topics?

- Are there any cross-curricular opportunities to consider?

- In subjects such as science and design technology, are there any safety considerations?

- How relevant is the curriculum to the context of the school and its pupils?

- What are the expectations of parents regarding subject content and skills progression?

- What adaptations would have to be made to enable non-specialists to deliver the curriculum effectively?

These are all questions which teachers will always have considered as part of their day-to-day teaching and planning but probably not in such explicit terms. The task now for middle leaders is the careful analysis of good practice and good intentions. They need to be able to explain the thinking behind their decisions and thus develop a clear rationale for the work of their departments. Drawing together the intentions of colleagues into a coherent approach to the teaching of a particular subject is indeed a challenge. The questions outlined above provide a good starting point and will enable leaders to shape a common approach to the curriculum. Such an approach provides the coherence needed in subject departments, or within primary settings, to ensure that all pupils benefit equally from high quality teaching.

The complexity of the notion of intent may seem somewhat overwhelming when set out a series of questions like those suggested above, but the discussions undertaken as a result are bound to be both stimulating and worthwhile. The introduction of the EIF has certainly thrown a spotlight on the work of middle leaders but it has also helped to ensure that colleagues across the country are discussing the curriculum in much more detail than ever before. This has not only helped to raise the status of middle leaders, but also will undoubtedly lead to much more joined-up thinking in subject areas and across schools.

Note

1 *School Inspection Handbook*, Handbook for inspecting schools in England under section 5 of the Education Act 2005, (2019); updated September 2019, Reference no: 190017, Crown copyright 2019, p. 26.

2

Do I have a vision for my subject?

Most schools now have a vision statement, and the need to develop one features strongly in training programmes for senior leaders. Many of these statements are little more than vague aspirational summaries full of good intentions. Most are values-based, highlighting characteristics such as perseverance and resilience, and very few focus specifically on teaching and learning. They usually aim to enable pupils, in the words of the cliché, 'to become the best version of themselves'. Departmental or subject visions can be more explicit and directly focused on teaching and learning.

I think it is true to say that most teachers enter the profession partly driven by the love of a subject. They may well be attracted to teaching per se, and they may have a wish to work with young people, but very few do not already have a passionate attachment to the subject they have spent three or more years studying at university. It is from this attachment that their subject vision originates. Whether it derives from an appreciation of the world's great literature, the wonder of scientific enquiry, or simply the sheer enjoyment of physical activity, what drives most teachers into the profession is the desire to pass on what they know and to share their enthusiasm for their particular subject. They want the children in their classes to experience the joy and fascination of English literature, or geography, or music. Put simply, they want to inspire them with a thirst for learning.

Having studied a subject in depth, teachers entering the profession already have a good idea of what they consider to be its most important aspects. It is these they will want to pass on. An understanding of the intersection between the needs of pupils and the fundamentals of a particular subject takes a while to develop. However, as they become more experienced, teachers begin to appreciate which aspects of the subject will be most relevant to their pupils, and which will be the most inspiring. Programmes of study and examination specifications may point the way in terms of relevance, but the inspirational aspects come from the teacher's own engagement with his or her subject area.

In this way, teachers develop a vision for passing on their subject knowledge. They may have never expressed it explicitly – they may not even have thought about it in these terms – but very few teachers lack a subject vision. The task of the subject leader is to explore the views of colleagues in order to shape a broader vision to be shared by all. This can be a demanding task in a large department in a secondary school which may have ten or more teachers, or in a primary setting where a subject is taught by everyone in the school, but a shared understanding is essential if the subject is to be a success.

As always, the starting point is a discussion. There will, of course, be general areas which everyone agrees are important. In the teaching of reading, for example, few would disagree with the need to develop fluency, or to facilitate the acquisition of a broad vocabulary. There will also be agreement with regard to what it is hoped children will get out of learning to read: a love of reading, the ability to communicate effectively, the skills they need to access learning in other subjects, etc. In effect, the basic vision for the subject is there already. The discussion becomes much more interesting, however, when the details begin to be explored. What is an appropriate balance between helping pupils develop the functional skills they need to communicate effectively, and simply reading for pleasure? In the teaching of writing, how much time should be spent on creative writing and how much on technical skills? In every subject, there will be similar issues to explore. In science, how much time should be spent on practical work aimed at stimulating pupils' interest in the subject in preference to teaching the more demanding formulae and equations which provide its underpinnings?

Such discussions tend to form a continuous dialogue across departments, across schools and, indeed, across the profession. In some cases, it is the ongoing nature of the discussion that provides the internal cohesion that departments need to thrive, and out of these discussions, vision for departments will begin to emerge. This process should never seem onerous – for most teachers, this is the very substance of education – and such discussions are much more interesting than management meetings looking at data or the calendar for next year.

There will of course come a point when the subject leader will need to articulate the department's vision. It may never have been written down, but good middle leaders develop a sound understanding of the views of their colleagues and are able to combine them with their own to shape a vision which is common to all. They are then ready to answer key questions:

- What is the importance of your subject, and why is it important for pupils to study it?
- How do you intend to inspire pupils with a love of learning in your subject?
- What are the skills you feel are essential?
- What do you hope pupils will gain from the subject?
- How will it equip them to navigate the world?

Most middle leaders will already feel confident that they can answer these questions. However, making them explicit is a really useful exercise. Following departmental discussions, it is worth taking the time to attempt to draft a written departmental vision to see if the aims and aspirations of one's colleagues can be captured. As we will see, an agreed vision is a good place to start when it comes to writing a curriculum statement. Moreover, the ability to talk confidently and with authority about the department's vision is a sure sign of a successful leader.

3

How do I work within the context of the whole school and address whole school priorities?

As we have seen, virtually all schools have vision statements, which seek to indicate the institution's overarching priorities. They are perforce very general, tremendously aspirational and, it is fair to say, usually ignored by the majority of staff. Although a great deal of time and effort goes into their construction, once decided upon they often end up as banners on the website and are thus quietly forgotten. Nevertheless, they do set the tone for the way the school operates and give a sense of what the place is all about. Subject vision statements are much more practical propositions, closely connected as they are to the day-to-day work of the classroom. However, they sit within the overall vision and are therefore necessarily subject to its influence.

For a more detailed account of a school's context and its priorities, one must turn first towards its website, and then the school improvement or development plan. A glance at the data gives a sense of a school's population – the proportion of pupil premium students or those with special educational needs, for example – and performance tables tell us about attainment and progress. Then, of course, there is the geographical location of the school: leafy suburb or deprived inner-city borough? However, it is the website and the development plan that really give a flavour of the school and its priorities.

Good schools have up to date, well presented websites which are easy to navigate and used regularly by parents and visitors. Their content allows the casual reader to quickly build up a picture of the life of the school, and the best ones impart a sense of activity and vibrance. Pictures of recent activities, trips and visits, lists of future projects, celebrations of important events, signposts to a wide range of learning opportunities etc. bring the place to life. Comprehensive information about the school day, about examinations, about the curriculum, staff, governors, and school improvement ambitions round out the image created in the mind. Of course, some of this can be considered as advertising fluff or hype (this is particularly the case with independent schools where commercial considerations predominate) but websites which are updated regularly tend to give a fairly accurate picture of what the school is really like.

They are also often indicative of the level of professionalism in the school. A carefully organised and comprehensive website may be regarded as simply a useful addition to the day-to-day operation of an institution, but it says a great deal about its context. A middle leader seeking to lead a department in a school with a disorganised, complacent and unenthusiastic management team will find his or her task much more challenging than in a professional and up-to-date establishment, where attention to detail is regarded as essential. Context isn't simply a matter of location and pupil population, it includes atmosphere and working conditions. Skilled middle leaders take this into account and attempt to shape their departments accordingly. This may mean simply working in line with the standards set by the senior leadership team or, in some cases, developing a superior set of standards. Exemplary middle leaders working in unprofessional environments often pave the way for others to follow, and in this way become key to successful school improvement.

The school development plan is, of course, where the school's priorities are set out explicitly. Good plans are constructed as a result of a careful review of the school's context and performance, and in consultation with staff. Their success can be measured not only in terms of outcomes, but also by the degree to which they are shared across the school. Plans which respond realistically to the needs of the school, without being overly optimistic or burdening, are likely to be welcomed by staff and followed as a result. Such plans provide a basic outline; it is then up to middle leaders to fill in the details.

Middle leaders therefore need to be familiar with the school's development plan and share its goals. Hopefully, they will have been party to its construction and therefore feel greater commitment towards its aims and objectives, but even if this is not the case the plan should offer a broad outline of the school's priorities for development. The major focus is usually on examination performance and curriculum development, and it is easy for middle leaders to work alongside their colleagues towards common goals such as these. If attainment is low across the board, for example, subject leaders will need to develop plans to improve attainment in their subject areas to ensure that the improvements they achieve are in line with attainment across the school. If the leadership team proposes significant restructuring of the curriculum, middle leaders will need to think carefully about how they re-shape their individual curriculum areas in order to align with the wider changes. In both cases, the management and deployment of staff will be key considerations. These two examples make it clear that subject leaders have to respond to the challenges set out in the plan, but it is probably true to say the challenges mirror those they have already set themselves. It is only when major changes are indicated – the wholesale restructuring of staff, for example – that middle leaders may find themselves working towards goals they may not share but nevertheless have to manage.

Subject leaders cannot operate in isolation. The choices they make and the actions they undertake must fit in with the work of their colleagues and the plans of senior leaders. Once they understand the general principles and the direction of travel they do, however, have considerable autonomy. Their choices have a profound influence on the curriculum and how it is taught, and they model leadership skills not only for the staff in their departments, but also for colleagues across the school. Good middle leaders understand the school's context and its priorities, they share the school's vision, but they also appreciate the fact that the work they do in departments is the real driver of school improvement.

4

What do I want pupils to be able to do by the end of the year?

This is another one of those questions where the answer at first seems obvious but then gathers complexity as the topic is explored. In responding to the question, a subject leader is likely to begin outlining the content to be covered by the end of the year. In Key Stages 1 and 3, this will relate to National Curriculum programmes of study, or the schemes of work based upon them; in Key Stages 2, 4 and 5, the focus will be on the content of tests and examinations. There is a fixed amount of content to cover, and it is therefore simply divided up across the years. To answer the question, all that is needed, one would assume, is the ability to list the topics covered and provide an explanation for the choice of the final topic, or end of year assessment. This, however, is just the starting point.

The choice of content needs to be considered. Very few teachers attempt to cover every aspect of the National Curriculum programmes of study – there simply isn't the time – and there is bound to be some degree of selection with regard to preparation for examinations. At the very least, some topics will be allocated more time than others. The nature of the cohort is also a significant factor: delivery of the curriculum will need to be adapted to suit the learning needs of the pupils in the classroom. A highly selective grammar school is unlikely to follow the same schemes of work as an inner-city comprehensive school serving a deprived area. The question then becomes, 'How much content do I need to cover, and in what depth?'

The order in which topics are taught is also a factor here. This idea is covered in detail in the second part of this book, where the importance of sequencing is explored, but it is essential to recognise that curriculum intentions are often shaped by the order in which topics are taught. If subject leaders have a particular end point in mind, each stage of the journey needs to be carefully planned. They then need to be able to articulate and justify the choices they have made.

Nor is the question simply a matter of content. It is also a matter of skills and understanding. A subject leader may well be asked, 'What do you want pupils to understand by the end of the year?'

Again, this is a complex question. There will undoubtedly be certain skills that teachers need their pupils to master in order to gain a greater understanding of the subject, but it is difficult to simply list them. A teacher of modern languages might suggest that by the end of Year 7, pupils need to be familiar with the use of verbs in the present tense, and a science teacher might require them to be able perform practical experiments safely and according to the scientific method, but these are skills which develop over time. Pupils' understanding grows and they become more skilled as they move up through the school. At best, teachers can hope to have enabled pupils to begin to understand the skills, ideas and concepts they are trying to impart.

If we turn to the teaching of reading, for example, it becomes almost impossible to say exactly what it is hoped pupils will understand by the end of the year. Progress in reading is notoriously difficult to predict. Most teachers would probably respond to the question by resorting to vague suggestions. Pupils should have developed fluency, or they should have acquired a wide vocabulary, but what does fluency really mean, and what exactly is a wide vocabulary? It may be possible to specify a list of words to be learnt by the end of each term, and to suggest a number of books to have achieved under a reading scheme, but pupils learn at different rates, and such concrete targets soon become meaningless. How, then, should the question be answered?

The most convincing answers are likely to recognise that learning is an uneven process and that end points are aspirations rather than targets. Instead of insisting that pupils will know a hundred key words and have reached level five of the reading scheme, for example, experienced subject leaders will focus on the development of skills and understanding. By the end of the year the following topics will have been covered (in this sequence for these reasons) in order to enable pupils to acquire this knowledge and to begin to develop, or learn to enhance, these skills. They will begin to acquire an understanding of these ideas and concepts, and, above all, they will be enjoying their learning and appreciating its significance.

Of course, the end of the term or the end of the year isn't a simple cut-off point. It is also important to think about preparing pupils for what comes next. What subject content, what skills and ideas will they need, to be able to move on successfully to the next stage of their education? Such considerations form a key part of the teaching around transition points when pupils are being prepared to move up from primary to secondary school, for example, or from GCSE to A-Level, but they are equally important as they move up through the school. Will enough content have been covered? Will the right ideas and skills have been taught? and will pupils have developed sufficient understanding to be able to continue to flourish when they move up from Year 3 to Year 4, or Year 8 to Year 9?

Once problems of content and skills acquisition have been considered, the issue of challenge arises. Challenge has become something of a buzzword in discussions of pedagogy, and it will certainly be explored as part of the inspection process, but it is also key to the notion of intent. Middle leaders are encouraged to ensure that their pupils are offered sufficient challenge to ensure that they make strong progress. This enables the weakest to be supported and move on, and the brightest to fulfil their potential and not get bored. There is very little to object to in the concept of a challenging curriculum; it is in the degree of challenge where difficulties emerge. There is absolutely no point in designing a curriculum that attempts to push pupils forward at a pace they simply cannot manage; nor is there any value in creating one that moves so slowly that even the weaker pupils get bored by the pace of the work. I have visited English departments where texts such as O'Brien's *Mrs Frisby and the Rats of NIMH* – a book most Year 4 or 5 pupils would be comfortable reading – is taught to mixed ability Year 7 classes, resulting in bored, dispirited pupils who quickly lose interest in the subject. On the other hand, it is not uncommon for teachers to attempt to deliver in full demanding texts such as *King Lear* in Year 7 to showcase their 'take no prisoners' approach to challenge. Getting the balance right is key to a successful curriculum. It is dependent upon a thorough understanding of the school's context and the nature of its intake, but it must also take into account the aspirations of the school's vision and development plan. Skilled middle leaders understand their pupils and tailor the degree of challenge accordingly.

Similarly, thought must be given to pupils who are unlikely to reach their targets by the end of the year, those whose understanding falters, those who are unable to absorb the content covered, and those who cannot grasp the concepts delivered. Curriculum intent must therefore ensure that 'catch-up' is built in. The question, 'What do I want children to have learnt by the end of the year?' must acknowledge that children learn at different rates. In answering this question, middle leaders need to recognise that their response is likely at first to be very general – an ambition for the majority. The answer will then need further thought to consider how it applies to groups and individuals. It is here that a really sophisticated approach is required.

Sketching out the content, skills and concepts to be achieved by the end of the year thus becomes something of an umbrella which reaches out over everyone in the class or year group. Under that umbrella, there will be pupils with special educational needs who have every right to experience the same curriculum, and for whom expectations should be equally as high as for all other pupils in the class, but who may well struggle with some aspects of the learning. The consideration of their progress is a key aspect of the notion of curriculum intent. Pupils from disadvantaged backgrounds may lack the cultural capital to engage fully with some aspects of the curriculum, and this therefore also becomes something to consider when thinking about what pupils are expected to have learnt by the end of the year. The same applies to all groups, whether this means pupils with English as an additional language, or those who are especially gifted in the subject.

In considering the complexity of the question, 'What do I want children to have learnt by the end of the year?' it is, of course, impossible to avoid consideration of tests and examinations. If young people are taking public examinations, they must be properly prepared, and middle leaders must ensure that the curriculum covers all that is necessary for examination success. However, as we have seen, a strong curriculum is not simply a list of examination topics. Examinations are the end point of years of learning, but they do not test pupils' understanding of everything they have learnt during their schooling. A strong subject curriculum is much more than a journey towards an examination.

Of course, examinations – especially internal examinations or assessments – are an important part of the learning process, and they enable teachers to gauge the depth of the learning that has taken place. A key aspect of curriculum intent, therefore, is the effectiveness of teaching in bringing about the learning. To that end, it is important for leaders to ask, 'How secure is pupils' learning?' An imaginative and challenging curriculum cannot be considered successful if pupils forget most of it, or are unable to demonstrate the skills they should have acquired during the course of the year. The role of assessment in supporting the curriculum is considered in more detail in the second part of this book, but it is important at this stage to recognise its importance to the notion of intent. In essence, it is a question of evaluation. If leaders have a good idea of what they want pupils to have learnt and understood by the end of the year, they will also need to have thought about how they will evaluate the success of their plans.

Leaders also need to ensure that the teachers in their departments or subject areas are ready to hand on their classes to other teachers. It is standard practice in most schools, whether secondary or primary, for classes to have a different subject teacher each year, especially in larger settings. It is therefore essential that pupils in different classes have reached the same stage in the curriculum so that the next teacher knows exactly where to begin at the start of the new year. Consistency is therefore important to a subject's success, and is something that will be certainly looked for under any inspection regime. One could argue that, as a teacher, to be worth one's salt involves quickly getting to know a new class and then deciding where to begin, but the transition process is so much easier in departments with common goals and working patterns. In these departments, pupils are much less likely to fall behind in their learning or miss key aspects of the curriculum.

Ultimately, of course, by the end of the year, not only will middle leaders have ensured that pupils have developed a good understanding of the skills and concepts required to move on to the next stage of their learning, but also they will above all have helped to inspire them to continue learning.

5

How do I identify areas for improvement?

There are three strands to consider in the identification of areas for improvement. First, as we have seen, there is the whole school development plan. This will outline the general areas for improvement which individual subjects must work towards. These are usually performance or curriculum related and, more often than not, result in departments setting themselves the goal of improving both progress and attainment, or simply maintaining current standards, in order to fall in line with whole school objectives. Second, there are the issues identified by the department which clearly need improvement. This might include performance in a particular topic or examination paper, changes to schemes of work, revised setting arrangements, refinements to marking and feedback etc. These are improvements which will undoubtedly help to bring about the objectives of the whole school plan, but which are essentially subject based. Third, there is all the other stuff, the day-to-day items which need revising, updating, simplifying or just generally sorting out. It might be a question of organising the stock cupboard, improving shared resources, supervising new or temporary staff or adapting to new examination specifications.

Effective middle leaders constantly evaluate the work of their departments. They recognise that the departmental or subject evaluations led by members of the senior leadership team – in other words, the school's accountability mechanisms – tell only part of the story. Work must be done in response to these mechanisms, but much more is required for leaders to ensure that they really understand the strengths and weaknesses of the departments they lead. Formal monitoring meetings with senior staff are likely to cover examination performance and the monitoring of the quality of teaching and learning in the classroom, but they will only occasionally touch upon the complexities of day-to-day management. Of course, the two are intimately connected: strong leaders who constantly look for ways to improve every aspect of their own and their colleagues' work will find it much easier to satisfy the demands of the senior leadership team. As always, attention to detail is the most effective way to bring about more general improvements.

Good middle leaders know what needs improving; making their ideas explicit is more challenging. Explaining how they know what needs improving is even more difficult. So, how do successful middle leaders go about identifying areas for improvement, and what evidence do they draw on?

Examination and test performance are the obvious places to start. Analysis of pupils' performance in each topic or individual paper reveals the areas where they did well or struggled. Complacent leaders may dream up a raft of excuses for poor performance – a weaker cohort, more demanding examination questions, too many temporary staff etc. – and simply hope that things will get better next year. More competent leaders will take such issues into account, but then forensically examine the performance of pupils in each paper to indicate areas of weakness in curriculum provision. These are then discussed in departments or subject teams, explored in lesson monitoring visits, reviewed by reference to pupils' work in books, and so on. It may be that the results have been skewed by poor curriculum decisions, or by weaker teaching. The key point, of course, is that only by accurate identification of areas of weakness can anything be done to put things right. More to the point, weaknesses have to be acknowledged before they can be corrected. The old adage, 'weak teachers blame the pupils, but strong teachers blame themselves', is not too far off the mark.

Lower down the school, where public examination data is not always available, the same rigour needs to be applied to internal assessments, but these may not always be as reliable as one would like. More emphasis must therefore be given to what is usually described as soft data, but which can be as precise as that provided by detailed examination analysis. Careful discussion of each curriculum topic by the teachers concerned is bound to illuminate its strengths and weaknesses. Such discussions should therefore form a regular part of department and subject meetings. It is also important to consider pupils' response to the topics taught: Is their enjoyment obvious? What is the impact on their behaviour for learning? Is the work they produce in class of a high quality? Pupil voice may be key here: if conducted with care, discussions with pupils can tell you more about the subject, the department and the school, than any method of statistical analysis.

The effective monitoring of the work of teachers in the classroom will be explored in detail later in this book, but it is vital that subject leaders know the strengths and weaknesses of the staff in their departments. The only way to do this is to spend time with them in their classrooms. This is always a tricky subject, and the whole area of teacher observation is something of a minefield, but lesson observation doesn't have to be punitive. In the best departments, teachers work as a team and share ideas; lesson observations are regarded as part of the sharing process. Of course, teachers understand that middle leaders are accountable to the headteacher and therefore have to evaluate their performance on a regular basis, but if this becomes part of the day-to-day sharing of good practice, rather than as a result of isolated formal visits, then tensions lessen, and genuine collaboration takes place. In this way, middle leaders will be able to identify areas of weakness, share examples of good practice, and thus make improvements much more effectively. Good leaders do not shy away from lesson visits, and they are not afraid to have honest conversations where weaknesses are apparent.

Another important means of identifying areas for improvement is by external evaluation. Examination performance is obviously part of this process, but successful middle leaders are usually open to support from other departments, other schools, and external advisers. There is much to be learnt from the good practice of other middle leaders. A head of maths may perhaps feel that he or she has little to learn from what goes on in the English department, but pedagogy is universal and not restricted to individual subjects. If a subject leader is improving pupil performance by an innovative approach, then this approach should surely be shared. It may not be directly transferrable from one subject to another, but it could perhaps be adapted. More often than not, however, it can be adopted wholesale and pupils will benefit as a result. The days of subject departments as exclusive enclaves or walled cities are long gone.

Similarly, middle leaders should be encouraged to visit departments in other schools to explore good practice. They don't necessarily have to be outstanding departments: there is something to learn from every visit to another school. It is also important for colleagues to explore other phases of education. Strong leaders in secondary schools want to know what works in primary classrooms, and primary subject leaders should ensure that they understand how their subject is taught at secondary level.

Finally, it is often useful to seek support from external advisers. Though very few are employed directly by local authorities nowadays, there are still dozens of educational consultants offering their services to schools. They have to be chosen carefully – usually as a result of personal recommendation – but they often have a wealth of experience and a knowledge of good practice from a wide range of other schools. They may be commissioned by senior leaders to help identify issues in underperforming departments, but successful middle leaders request their services because they recognise that even the best departments can be improved. External advisers also include inspectors, of course. Areas for improvement feature in inspection reports, though under the new framework they are limited and general in nature, but the conversations middle leaders have with inspectors during whole school inspections can offer valuable insights into departmental improvement.

6

How do I write a curriculum statement?

A curriculum statement is not a curriculum plan (see below). A plan maps out in detail what pupils will be learning in each year as they move up through the school; a curriculum statement offers a general overview of the subject intended to give readers a clear idea of how it is taught in the school, and the context in which it is taught. It is, of course, aimed at parents, and should be written in an appropriate style. This doesn't mean the 'Janet and John' style of the latest inspection reports – Ofsted report writing guidance suggests that reports should aim for a reading age of nine or ten – but that the writing must be clear and accessible.

There should, of course, be a whole school curriculum statement and, as with the development plan, a departmental or subject statement should conform to the general outlines it provides. It will, however, be more detailed and more specific, and it should begin with a summary of the school's vision for the subject.

As we have seen, a subject leader will have a vision for his or her subject, though it may not have been formalised in a written statement. It is hoped, however, that it will have formed a part of regular departmental or subject team discussions. It is therefore useful to introduce a subject curriculum statement with a brief outline of this vision and perhaps some indication of why the subject is important. Literacy, reading and numeracy at primary level; English, maths and science in secondary schools; these subjects have a head start as parents naturally see these subjects as forming the core of the educational experience. Other subjects may have to work harder to create a sense of the subject's importance; a strong vision must therefore be convincing and relevant.

Parents will want to see an outline of the broad sweep of the subject as it develops across the school. How, for example, will the phonics taught in Reception prepare children to become increasingly fluent readers in Key Stage 1? How will the teaching of maths in Year 7 build upon the numeracy skills acquired in Key Stage 2? And how will the subject prepare pupils for GCSEs and beyond? The obvious way to do this is by providing an outline of what happens in each Key Stage, with an indication of the public tests and examinations pupils will be prepared for.

It is also important to talk about how the subject is taught. Is the approach formal or informal? Is it largely focused on practical work, or is a firm grounding in theory the starting point? Is group work encouraged, or is the focus on individual endeavour? Is the aim to ensure that pupils are prepared for tests and examinations at an early stage, or is a broader view of the subject encouraged? There is no need for a long exegesis on the department's approach to pedagogy, but it is important to impart a sense of what lessons will be like. It is also sensible to emphasise teachers' commitment to ensuring that pupils of all abilities are provided for and encouraged to flourish.

Although not strictly necessary, it is also useful to say something about the quality and professionalism of staff, as well as the facilities available. A subject leader with access to state-of-the-art facilities and a full team of highly trained subject specialists would be foolish to omit mention of these impressive facts. A final sentence focusing on the subject's strong record of examination success, or, in an underperforming department, a note about ambitions for future success, is likely to provide a very positive and uplifting conclusion.

To summarise, a comprehensive curriculum statement should include some or all of the following:

- An introductory summary of the school's vision for the subject.

- A comment on the subject's importance.

- A general outline of the subject as it grows and develops – from Reception to Year 6; from Year 7 to A-Level.

- An indication of how it builds upon what has gone before; how Year 7 builds upon Year 6, for example.

- A brief outline of what happens in each Key Stage.

- Some idea of the department's approach to teaching.

- A summary of the public examinations for which pupils are to be prepared – Key Stage tests, GCSEs, vocational qualifications, A-Levels.

- An indication of how pupils are prepared for what is to come – secondary schooling, university, or the world of work.

- Reference to the support provided for pupils of all abilities – SEND pupils, the most able etc.

- A brief indication of the extra-curricular activities aimed at enhancing pupils' experience of the subject.

- A summary of the facilities available to the subject, and a comment on how it is staffed.

- Some indication of the department's success.

7
How do I create a curriculum plan?

The subject curriculum plan builds upon the curriculum statement to offer an overview of the learning planned for each year group. It is not a fully-fledged scheme of work; it is a catalogue of the topics and skills teachers will be covering during the course of each term. In essence it is an overview of the year and serves; therefore, both as a guide for parents and a useful aide-memoire for class teachers. It doesn't need to be particularly detailed – the detail can be reserved for the schemes of work – but it should show clearly the topics to be covered, the skills to be learnt, and the sequence of learning. The better ones also include reference to cross-curricular skills such as literacy and numeracy; some include aspects of the personal, social and health education (PSHE) agenda, especially if it is school policy for such topics to be mapped across the curriculum and not delivered by discrete subject teaching.

Most plans follow the six-term structure, and most are set out in tabular form, with each half term presented as column headings. This is certainly the simplest and clearest way to present the situation. Fully worked examples are included in the appendix and a suggested outline is shown below. The headings of the rows vary from school to school, but it is good practice for schools to adopt a common format. This helps to ensure consistency across the school and makes collaboration between departments much easier.

Curriculum Plan – Y7 English

	Autumn 1	Autumn 2	Spring 1	Spring 2	Summer 1	Summer 2
Topic						
Topic Objectives						
Knowledge/Skills to be acquired						

(*Continued*)

	Autumn 1	Autumn 2	Spring 1	Spring 2	Summer 1	Summer 2
Assessment						
Links with prior/ subsequent learning						
Literacy/ Numeracy Skills						

The topic row simply comprises the titles of the units. Autumn 1 in Year 7, for example, is likely to include induction topics which assess and consolidate the work done in the primary phase and prepare pupils for what is to come. Similarly, Summer 2 in Year 6 is likely to cover topics which prepare pupils for their secondary education. The topic objectives state clearly what teachers intend their pupils to learn and experience, while the knowledge and skills section sets out the specific skills to be learnt. For example, an introductory unit in music may have objectives covering a particular genre – the aim being to familiarise pupils with the particular work of a composer perhaps, or begin to appreciate the complexity of orchestral music – but it is the next section which indicates the specific skills to be acquired, the basics of musical notation, perhaps, or the ability to recognise a range of different instruments.

The assessment row should be more than simply a list of tests to be conducted. It should set out clearly how teachers intend to check on pupils' learning. It could, of course, include end of unit tests, but it should also cover the activities teachers use on a day-to-day basis to assess the progress their pupils have been making in order to enable them to adapt or refine their teaching accordingly. It could therefore include essays, homework assignments, oral work, individual discussions with the teacher, practical assignments etc. Teachers will, of course, use a variety of methods in their teaching to check on learning, but it is important for there to be common assessments set out in the curriculum plan to enable moderation of standards across the department.

The final two rows are often missing from subject curriculum plans, but they are surely essential. Teachers who do not know what their pupils have learnt before they enter the classroom often start again from scratch. This not only impedes progress, but also engenders boredom and disaffection. Similarly, those who disregard the next stages of education may well neglect vital skills and knowledge, which means that pupils may not be properly equipped to cope with the new learning they will soon encounter. Highly effective middle leaders work hard to ensure that the teachers of their subject are fully aware of prior learning. Year 7 teachers should have a thorough understanding of the Year 6 curriculum, for example. Similarly, subject leaders should also ensure that staff are aware of what the next stage of education looks like. Primary teachers, for example, should be familiar with the demands of their subject at Key Stage 3, and even GCSE. Setting out what we might call the 'before and after' links in the curriculum statement ensures that teachers take a broader view and recognise that learning is a continuum from Reception to Year 13 and beyond, and is not restricted to the year group they are currently teaching.

Of course, there are difficulties here. Some secondary schools are served by dozens of primary feeder schools, making an understanding of exactly what pupils have learnt in Year 6 almost impossible. However, part of the work of a middle leader is to work with primary and secondary colleagues to identify common strands. The basics are in the National Curriculum programmes of study, but successful schools work hard not only to develop a consistent approach to the curriculum within school but to develop a shared approach across their family of schools. The inclusion of 'before and after' links on the curriculum plan ensures that teachers pay more than lip service to prior and subsequent learning.

Given the fact that literacy and numeracy skills are fundamental to a child's education, it is surprising that many subject plans do not include reference to them. In too many departments in secondary schools, teachers still regard literacy as the job of the English department, and numeracy skills are often ignored completely. In primary schools, these skills underpin almost every aspect of the curriculum and this should be the case at secondary level. Again, by including reference to them in the curriculum plan, middle leaders make it clear that they recognise the importance of these skills. One of the biggest barriers to examination success in maths, for example, is a candidate's inability to interpret the question. He or she may well be an excellent mathematician, but if the question is not understood, failure beckons.

As a writer sketches out the plot of a novel, dividing it into chapters or episodes, middle leaders plot the development of their subjects using curriculum plans. The final chapter of a novel may result in the capture of the villain or a happy marriage, but it is the way the story is told which engages and draws the reader in. A satisfying ending is important, but it is the story that counts. The curriculum plan sets out the story of a pupil's educational experience in a particular subject. The ending is, of course, defined by tests and examinations, but it is the story where real engagement takes place.

Having thought deeply about the story and how to tell it, it is up to middle leaders to put their ideas into practice. The first step is to make them visible.

8

How do I make my curriculum plans visible?

Too many curriculum statements and curriculum plans are created and then locked away in filing cabinets. Middle leaders need to ensure that these are live documents, and under constant review. The first step is to ensure that every subject teacher has a copy and that they are regularly discussed in department or subject team meetings. Some leaders create folders of reference material for their teams comprising key subject documentation, and these can be brought along to meetings to refer to and to update.

It is also important for pupils to understand the shape of their learning. It is good practice, therefore, to display copies of curriculum plans on the walls of the classroom. They may need editing, to redact sensitive comments, or simplifying, so that they are easier to understand, but they will be appreciated by pupils and give them a real sense of purpose. There is nothing worse than trying to learn something when one can't see the point of learning it. Pupils appreciate a secure sense of direction, and respond positively as a result of it.

Finally, plans should be available on the school website. Most schools now feature subject or department areas on their websites and middle leaders should take advantage of the opportunity to set out their stalls and provide the information parents look for. A subject page should include the curriculum statement, a list of staff who teach the subject (including, of course, support staff), and curriculum plans for each year group. Comprehensive websites also include examination specifications, links to additional resources, suggestions for wider reading, key vocabulary, and revision material. Whatever is included, however, must be kept up to date. It is a good idea to allocate responsibility for the website to one member of the team. Some departments regularly post updates which help to ensure that the website is read and checked regularly. These can take the form of subject news, the book of the month, the latest scientific discovery, a history post relating to a popular television programme etc. Lots of schools now display pupils' work – just as it is displayed on classroom walls – and there are some really imaginative approaches being explored across the country: online art galleries, video diaries, student reportage etc. A skilfully curated and up-to-date website is able to showcase a department and convey an air of professionalism which is inspiring to teachers, parents and pupils.

9

How do I choose what to teach?

The obvious answer is, of course, the National Curriculum, plus material for tests and examinations. Once again, it is not that simple. Choosing curriculum content is a complex activity which has a profound influence on the way pupils learn. By sticking rigidly to National Curriculum programmes of study, followed by content dictated by examination specifications, subject leaders are in danger of offering dull and uninspiring courses which dampen pupils' spirits and slow their learning. The aim must surely be to construct a curriculum which is comprehensive in its coverage of the subject but both entertaining and inspiring. Some might question the notion of entertaining pupils – they might see entertainment as a distraction from serious academic learning – but teachers who strike a balance between entertainment and instruction are far more likely to capture pupils' attention and kindle a real love of learning.

Academies do not have to follow the National Curriculum, so they have much more flexibility about what they choose to cover. However, they do have to teach a 'broad and balanced curriculum', including English, mathematics, science and religious education. This, of course, means that middle leaders have much greater choice in terms of both content and skills, particularly in non-examination years. However, this apparent freedom is, in reality, constrained by the steady march towards terminal tests and examination papers. Consequently, very few academies dispense with the National Curriculum entirely. Theoretically, a teacher in Year 3, or in Year 8, can teach whatever he or she wants, but in practice, pupils need to be taught the foundations on which test and examination syllabuses will eventually build. A teacher in Year 5 cannot teach without planning for the Key Stage 2 tests; a teacher in Year 9 must be aware of the skills and knowledge required by the GCSE specifications. Nevertheless, despite these constraints, there is a significant degree of flexibility. Skilled middle leaders can construct highly engaging and effective curriculum plans which fully cover the skills and content required by the examining boards, but which also inspire and delight.

Inspiration rarely features in the aims and objectives of instructional teaching, but it is absolutely fundamental to success. It is important, therefore, to choose subjects which pupils find engaging and thoroughly absorbing. It is too easy to choose a book from the stock cupboard to teach without asking the question, 'Is there a better book available?' There will certainly be financial constraints, but curriculum choice goes right back to the ordering of stock. Similarly, the science teacher who, for years, has taught titration with a tried and tested experiment, ought to be asking colleagues whether they have a practical activity which pupils enjoy more, and thus remember better. This is often a real issue at A-Level where staff tend to opt for safe choices of texts or topics – or those they themselves studied when they were in the sixth form – when much more inspiring choices are available. Busy English teachers may well choose a Jane Austen novel because they know it well and have studied it before, when there are other choices available which are much more likely to grab the attention of the young people in their classes.

Examination specifications usually offer a degree of choice in terms of topics and content. Admittedly, there is very little flexibility in the content of the Key Stage 2 tests, but GCSE and A-Level syllabuses usually offer a range of options. There is also the choice of different specifications offered by the various examination boards. Middle leaders need to consider such choices very carefully to ensure that they choose material relevant to their pupils, appropriate to the context of the school, and likely to achieve the best examination outcomes. As mentioned above, it is easy to fall back on choices dictated by familiarity, or the content of the stock cupboard, but effective leadership does not rely on custom and practice, it always seeks out the best way forward.

A key question to discuss at department or subject team meetings is, 'Which topics are most important?' It is too easy to say that they are all equally important; obviously they are not. Examination papers cover some areas in considerable depth while offering only the occasional question or reference to others. The whole syllabus has to be covered – teachers who neglect topics which rarely feature in past papers can become horribly unstuck if one is unexpectedly resurrected – but the length of time allocated to each topic needs to be carefully considered. This is where professional judgement is vital. How much time will be needed for pupils in this school, this cohort and, indeed, this class, to understand the topic fully? How much time should be taken to ensure that the topic is delivered in order to inspire and engage?

It is, of course, important for teachers to become fully conversant with the demands of tests and examinations, and it is the duty of the middle leader to ensure that they are. This means that the quirks and complexities of the various specifications must be regularly discussed and evaluated in department meetings and careful consideration must be given to continuous professional development (CPD). It is also useful for every department or subject team to have at least one teacher who works as an examiner for the syllabus in question to ensure up-to-date knowledge and a real understanding of how the papers are marked. The dominance of tests and examinations may be resented, and teachers will rightly protest that there is more to their subjects than terminal assessments, but middle leaders need to ensure that there is a high degree of examination expertise in their teams. Once this is in place, the curriculum can be planned and implemented in order to fulfil the wider ambitions of teachers. The National Curriculum and examination syllabuses are thus the foundations on which the curriculum is built but there are huge opportunities for imaginative embellishment as the final structure is put in place.

There are, of course, lots of practical questions to consider when deciding what to teach. First, there is the issue of resources. What resources are available? Is funding available to buy additional resources? Do new resources have to be made in-house, or are high quality commercial resources available? A department which continues to use an out of date textbook because staff are familiar with it, or it is all that can be afforded, is clearly disadvantaging pupils. It is important, therefore, for middle leaders to review the textbooks and equipment they have in their stock cupboards to see what needs updating and what needs throwing out. Sometimes, of course, there will simply not be enough money to enable departments to acquire high quality resources. In such cases, it will be necessary for teachers to adapt existing resources. In other words, to make the best of a bad lot. This undoubtedly creates additional work, but it has to be done.

One of the most difficult tasks middle leaders have to undertake is ensuring that students are well resourced. This means keeping up to date, presenting senior leaders and governors with the information they need to make sensible budgeting decisions, and, above all, pressing their subject or department's case. Leaders who understand the constraints on the budget, and who recognise that their colleagues in other departments are competing for the same pot of money with equally valid requests, are much more likely to succeed if their requests are reasonable, presented clearly, and accompanied by evidence of potential impact in the classroom. Ultimately, however, the availability of resources is a key consideration when planning what to teach. Some topics may not be taught effectively if the appropriate resources are unavailable. When things like this happen, the leader's vision for his or her subject is forced to face the stark realities of life in a chronically underfunded education system. This means that skilled leadership is essential if staff are to be supported, and pupils not disadvantaged.

Similarly, the nature of current staffing has to be taken into account. There is no point in designing a highly technical curriculum which demands a great deal of subject knowledge if the staff available to deliver it are non-specialists. Again, there is a careful balance to be struck to ensure that pupils are well taught. It may be that some topics can be simplified, or the time spent on their delivery truncated, so that more time is available for the topics where staff feel more confident and can be supported more effectively. Of course, leaders may need to ensure that the skills and topics covered in this way are returned to further up the school when specialist staffing may become available. In shaping a successful curriculum, it is therefore vital for leaders to think not just about content but about who will be delivering the content. A fully staffed department with experienced specialist teachers is something of a luxury nowadays. It is much more likely that there will be a mixture of specialists, non-specialists, newly or recently qualified teachers, and supply staff. Wise middle leaders therefore take staffing into account in the construction of the curriculum.

With so many constraints on curriculum provision – the National Curriculum, examinations, availability of resources, staffing etc. – it is easy to overlook the fact that the most important people involved here are the pupils on the receiving end. We have touched upon the importance of inspiration, and the necessity of ensuring that pupils are well prepared for their tests and examinations, but it is also important to consider whether the curriculum will enable them to learn and thrive. The importance of challenge is considered below, but the ability of pupils to cope with the skills and topics included in the curriculum should be a key consideration when middle leaders plan what to teach. There is no point including a topic at a particular point in the year if pupils end up struggling with it. Much better to include it at a later date when they have acquired the necessary skills and background knowledge – or simply the maturity – to cope with it. Middle leaders therefore need to be acutely aware of the strengths and weaknesses of the cohort for whom the curriculum is being planned. The overall ability of the group – and, indeed, the range of ability within the group – may well determine what can be taught and when. As we shall see, not only is the choice of topics important, but also the sequence in which they are taught key to a successful curriculum.

Before we move on to consider sequencing, there are some less obvious things to think about when deciding what to teach. Cross-curricular planning, for example. There is a tendency in secondary schools for subjects to see themselves as islands. The contact between, say, the history and science departments may be minimal, but effective middle leaders do not isolate themselves and are always ready to take what is happening elsewhere in the school into account. Of course, some subject areas lend themselves more easily to cross-curricular provision – literacy and numeracy are the obvious examples – but it is important for pupils to understand that their learning is not a question of disconnected chunks of information, but part of a wider picture. If subject leaders are unaware of what is being taught in other parts of the school, they may be missing opportunities to extend and deepen the learning in their own subject areas. Effective middle leaders, therefore, talk to their colleagues and seek out potential links when curriculum planning.

Secondary school teachers can learn a lot from their primary counterparts with regard to cross-curricular links. The delivery of foundation subjects at Key Stages 1 and 2 is often via topic books which draw together key ideas from a range of subjects. Work on Islam, for example, may be described as a religious studies topic, but it is likely to include elements of history and geography, and may well include practical skills from art and design. It will also, of course, include a great deal of work on literacy. Taking a holistic approach to curriculum planning undoubtedly enhances pupils' learning and enables them to understand the significance of that learning much more clearly.

Curriculum design also depends on a good understanding of the school's local context. In its simplest form, the planning of the curriculum takes into account local history, visits to places of interest, theatre trips etc. Rather than simply organising a trip to see whatever is playing at the nearest theatre, for example, if plans are made early enough, pupils will get to see the play they are studying in class while they are studying it, and the impact it will have on their learning will undoubtedly be much greater.

Finally, in this section, it is hard to underestimate the importance of literacy in deciding what to teach. Literacy underpins every subject in the curriculum, and it is a foolish middle leader who neglects to highlight its importance. Every opportunity should be taken to ensure that the literacy skills required to understand fully the topics being delivered are built into the learning.

10

What is meant
by 'sequencing'?

The term 'sequencing' is not new, but has gained prominence thanks to the new Ofsted framework. Like many technical terms, it is essentially a useful way of describing something which could easily be seen as common sense. In terms of the curriculum, it simply means that we need to think about the order in which things are taught. Obvious, yes, but, as we have seen, simple ideas often reveal remarkable depth once we really start to think about them.

In the January 2019 *School Inspection Update*, Sean Harford, Ofsted's National Director of Education, explains the concept of sequencing very clearly. He begins by pointing out the importance of connected learning:

> It is unhelpful to think of pupils' minds as 'empty vessels' waiting to be filled with isolated, disconnected pieces of information. People learn new knowledge when new concepts are connected in their minds with what they have already learned.
>
> It is more appropriate, therefore, to understand the way knowledge is stored as a complex, interconnected web or 'schema'. Every time a pupil encounters a word they have previously learned, but applied in a new context, it adds to the complexity of their understanding of that concept. In other words, they develop a deeper understanding of that concept and enhance their capacity to use that concept in their own thinking.[1]

This, of course, means that prior learning is used to help make connections and strengthen the web of learning:

> Where pupils lack prior knowledge, they may find it difficult to learn new knowledge or skills, because their short-term, working memory is likely to become temporarily overloaded. If they are able to draw on their long-term memory and attend to a small number of new features in what they are learning, they are much more likely to learn and make progress.[2]

In practice, most teachers are aware that learning has to be sequential if concepts are to be understood and skills acquired successfully. There is little point teaching children their times tables if their basic knowledge of number is uncertain, for example. However, it is surprising how disconnected many of the topics in subject curriculum plans actually are in practice. Primary colleagues will be familiar with the ways in which pupils jump from topic to topic in foundation subjects: one week they could be studying the Romans; the next they have jumped to Victorian England. There are, of course, particular chronological issues in the teaching of history but the same pattern occurs in many subject areas. In secondary schools, students often find themselves reading a completely unconnected series of novels and plays which have been chosen simply to satisfy the demands of the National Curriculum. They might find themselves studying Magorian's *Goodnight Mr. Tom* before moving straight on to a Shakespeare play. Inevitably, when the sequence of learning becomes random, pupils get confused and undoubtedly learning becomes less effective.

We have already discussed the importance of endpoints. Teachers and leaders must know where the curriculum is heading and what they want pupils to have learnt by the end of the year but, to make sure that the learning flows smoothly, they must also think about the order in which things are taught so that skills and knowledge build up step by step. Again, this is explained clearly in the *School Inspection Update*:

> New knowledge and skills do not exist in isolation, but rather build on what pupils already know and can already do. The order in which knowledge and skills are taught is therefore important. Since knowledge exists in rich schemata, an effective curriculum ensures that pupils are taught concepts and skills in an order that enables them to make useful connections that are not misapprehensions. This is what Ofsted understands by appropriate sequencing in the curriculum.

> There are serious consequences for pupils when a curriculum is not sequenced or designed effectively. Gaps in pupils' knowledge accumulate as they become layered on top of one another in a curriculum sequence. This accumulation of gaps, known as dysfluency, limits pupils' ability to acquire the complex skills that depend on them, and may even prevent them entirely from gaining those skills. This problem is sometimes called 'cumulative dysfluency'.[3]

The gaps are important. How many subject leaders think carefully about what has been missed when they plan a sequence of learning? More to the point, how many of them think about what could be missed if material is sequenced poorly?

Of course, sequencing does not imply a strict chronology. Sometimes it is better for pupils to change to a new, perhaps unrelated topic to ensure they stay fully engaged in their learning. But isn't this a break in the sequence, one might ask? It is a break in the immediate sequence, yes, but as long as the new learning builds upon prior learning there is still a sequence in place. Problems arise when the new learning assumes skills and knowledge which pupils don't have. To pick up on my earlier example, the jump from *Goodnight Mr. Tom* to Shakespeare might make perfect sense in a curriculum where both texts build on prior learning and both head towards a secure curriculum endpoint. This kind of curriculum planning is known as interleaving.

Notes

1 Harford, S. (2019). *School Inspection Update – January 2019 Special Edition* 180119. Crown Copyright 2019. www.gov.uk/government/organisations/ofsted. p.5.
2 Ibid. p.5.
3 Ibid. p.6.

11
What is interleaving?

Interleaving refers to the benefits of sequencing learning tasks so that similar items – two examples of the same concept, say – are interspersed with different types of items, rather than being consecutive. This results in more variable and challenging tasks but also offers benefits in terms of memory and the transfer of knowledge.[1]

It is important for pupils not to become bored and thus disengaged, and, as all teachers know, if too much time is spent on one topic or one skill, pupils lose interest and the pace of learning slows. Interleaving ensures that it is still possible to take a step by step approach, but that sufficient variety is injected into the learning to keep pupils engaged and, hopefully, inspired. Interleaving contrasts with the 'block' approach wherein similar items are taught together to achieve a kind of universal coverage. This, undoubtedly, offers the benefit of ensuring comprehensive coverage of a topic but it is likely to lead to some very bored pupils.

Interleaving has benefits in terms of spacing. There is research to suggest that knowledge and skills are learnt more easily when spaced out.[2] Trying to learn everything all at once, or in one go, can be difficult. Returning to a skill or block of knowledge a little later helps not only to secure it in the memory, but also makes the next steps easier to accomplish. The key point about interleaving, however, is that the gaps between teaching episodes should contain related material. The teacher may decide to switch to another topic before returning to the first one, but the new topic should not be completely unrelated. In this way, the curriculum can progress step by step but with real variety and strong connectedness.

Notes

1 Kang S. (2016). *The benefits of interleaved practice for learning.* In: Horvath J, Lodge J, and Hattie J (eds) *From the Laboratory to the Classroom: Translating Science of Learning for Teachers.* London: Routledge, pp. 79–93.
2 See, for example: Cepeda N, Vul E, Rohrer D, et al. (2008) Spacing effects in learning a temporal ridgeline of optimal retention. *Psychological Science* 9(11): 1095–1102.

12

How do I plan for progression?

The shift from attainment to progress as the key pupil performance measure had a significant impact on the way we think about the curriculum. When performance tables and Ofsted inspections focused on attainment, school leaders had to spend a great deal of time analysing, and indeed predicting, examination outcomes. The results of tests at Key Stages 1, 2 and 3, GCSEs and A-Levels were the main criteria by which schools were judged. Of course, skilled middle and senior leaders were acutely aware of the fact that performance at Key Stage 2 depends upon building solid foundations in the early years, and good GCSE results are only possible if the Key Stage 3 curriculum is well-planned, but their attention was certainly directed away from day-to-day progress towards terminal examinations.

Ofsted's definition of progress is, thankfully, very simple. It draws upon cognitive psychology and specifically research into long-term memory:

> If nothing has altered in long-term memory, nothing has been learned. Progress, therefore, means knowing more (including knowing how to do more) and remembering more. When new knowledge and existing knowledge connect in pupils' minds, this gives rise to understanding. As pupils develop unconscious competence and fluency, this will allow them to develop skills, i.e. the capacity to perform complex operations, drawing on what is known.

> Given the understanding of the curriculum set out above, progress should not be defined primarily by meeting standards or hitting the next data point. Rather, learning the curriculum itself is progress. If pupils attain within a well-sequenced, well-constructed curriculum, they are making progress.[1]

The inclusion of progress scores in national performance tables, and Ofsted's enlightened approach to the use of data, has meant that school leaders now focus much more closely on progress. This is surely a good thing and has led to a sea change in the ways in which lessons are monitored, pupils' work scrutinised, and assessment systems designed. Consequently, middle leaders need to think much more carefully about progress. Now that inspectors are not looking at internal data, the only way they can gauge pupil progress effectively is to look closely at what is happening in lessons. This means that middle leaders must attempt to ensure that pupils make progress in every lesson and not just by the end of the year or the course. Planning for progress is therefore key to the successful design and delivery of the curriculum. It also means that middle leaders need to be much more aware of what members of their teams are doing in their classrooms. In other words, they must be monitoring teaching quality on a regular basis, looking closely at pupils' work, and checking to ensure that school and department policies are being followed, particularly with regard to marking and assessment.

The first step is to ensure that progress is planned for and built into the curriculum. This necessitates an understanding of pupils' starting points, plus a realistic but ambitious estimate of their likely endpoints. Primary schools undoubtedly find it difficult to make accurate judgements regarding starting points. Children join schools from nurseries, child minders, and from home, and as a result, their early education varies enormously. The Early Years Foundation Stage Profile is supposed to give a clear picture of a child's starting points but there is scope for significant variation across schools. Primary heads, for example, are often accused of underestimating the abilities of children in Reception in order to show greater progress by the time they reach Key Stage 2. Similarly, secondary teachers regularly claim that pupils in Year 7 enter the school well below expected standards despite the fact that their Key Stage 2 results suggest that this is not the case.

It is up to middle leaders, therefore, to make their own judgements and to attempt to determine pupils' starting points as accurately as possible. In a way, it doesn't really matter if such assessments are not entirely accurate; what matters is the steps that are planned to ensure that progress is continuous and that pupils fulfil their potential. Teachers quickly gain a good understanding of their pupils' abilities, and how well they will do, and it is their assessments that should guide the initial learning steps. Key Stage tests should be borne in mind – and these are usually reinforced by the use of commercial tests such as CATS or NFER assessments – but teacher assessments a few weeks into the year are likely to give the most accurate results. Of course, this flies in the face of the Department for Education's thinking, where trust in teachers is negligible to say the least, but in the real world of the classroom, teachers do indeed know best.

This means that middle leaders need to pay particular attention to the first few weeks of their curriculum plans to allow a degree of flexibility, to enable teachers to get to know the pupils in their classes and gauge not only the ability, but also the learning potential, of each child. Thereafter, planning must take into account the need for a step by step approach which offers both support and challenge. The National Curriculum programmes of study offer a loose guide to progress at each stage and the estimates of key endpoints signal the destination, but close attention should be given to the stops along the way. Middle leaders therefore need to think carefully, as mentioned above, about sequencing and interleaving to ensure that each topic leads on to the next, and builds upon the one before. A well-planned curriculum provides the scaffold for effective teaching with opportunities for making progress built in at every stage. How quickly pupils make progress, of course, depends upon a range of factors including their ability, their background, and the quality of teaching. As we shall see, the curriculum also needs, therefore, to offer regular opportunities for assessment to enable catch-up and reinforcement of learning to take place. Planning for progress is far from straightforward, but an awareness of its importance is fundamental to good curriculum design.

Note

1 Harford, S. (2019). *School Inspection Update – January 2019 Special Edition* 180119. Crown Copyright 2019. www.gov.uk/government/organisations/ofsted. p.5.

13

How important is transition to my planning?

As we have seen, teachers use information provided by the previous stages in a pupil's education to help them plan the next. However, it is important to look beyond the data. Just as the content taught in previous lessons helps to prepare pupils for what they are about to learn, the content of the work done in previous years and settings shapes their learning as they move up through the school. It is essential, therefore, for teachers to have a good understanding of what is required of pupils at every stage of their education.

Most schools nowadays have comprehensive transition programmes which help support children as they move up from primary to secondary education. They visit their new school, meet the teachers, learn about the new routines and expectations, and get a flavour of what lessons will be like. Subject transition is much more hit and miss. Some teachers have a really good understanding of what went on in Year 6; others begin Year 7 completely oblivious of what has gone before. In many schools, it has long been common practice for teachers simply to start from scratch, particularly in foundation subjects. The impact of this is effectively to negate prior learning. It opens up a huge progress gap between Key Stages 2 and 3, and inevitably leads to a slower pace of learning.

Middle leaders who regard the curriculum as a continuum – from Reception to Year 13 – are much more likely to design effective subject curriculum plans. If they have a good knowledge of what pupils were learning in Year 6, they can build upon prior learning much more effectively. The easiest way to do this is to ensure that every teacher is familiar with the National Curriculum Programmes of Study for Key Stage 2, and for teachers of English and mathematics to have a good understanding of the content of the Key Stage 2 tests, but experienced middle leaders work to build strong links with their primary colleagues to gain a more detailed understanding of exactly what has been learnt. As we have seen, this can be difficult in secondary schools fed but ten or more primary schools, but closer links should nevertheless be attempted. The introduction of multi-academy trusts has perhaps made this easier to achieve, but even where primary schools have little contact with one another – as can be the case in rural areas – it should be the aim of secondary colleagues to find out as much as they can about the topics and skills taught in Years 5 and 6.

Of course, transition works both ways. It is similarly important for primary colleagues to have a good understanding of Key Stage 3, and indeed, GCSE. This will enable them to plan not only for Years 5 and 6, but for future learning. It will also ensure that extension activities for brighter pupils are relevant and of use to them when they move up to Year 7. The best curriculum plans even include an outline of learning undertaken in the previous or next school. So, a Key Stage 2 curriculum plan might cover Years 5, 6 and 7; a secondary subject plan might begin with Year 6.

14

How do I meet the needs of SEND and disadvantaged pupils?

Even in schools which have carefully designed curriculum plans, it can be difficult to ensure that the needs of all pupils are met. All pupils should have access to the entire curriculum, and long gone are the days when pupils with special needs were assumed not to be able to follow the same schemes of work as their peers. The curriculum sets out what is to be taught and when, but it should be planned with an awareness of all pupils in mind. This will make the teacher's job in adapting it to suit differing needs much more straightforward. This does not mean that the planned learning should be limited due to concerns over whether particular pupils will be able fully to participate; it does mean, however, that some thought should be given from the outset as to how the learning can be adapted. Ultimately it is up to the classroom teacher, perhaps working with the Special Educational Needs Co-ordinator (SENCO) or a teaching assistant, to make the adaptations which will make the learning more accessible, but careful curriculum planning makes this process not only more straightforward but a regular feature of lesson planning.

Disadvantaged pupils are not necessarily lower ability pupils, but they may well have particular needs to be taken into account when implementing the curriculum. They may have missed out on a significant amount of learning. It is therefore important that opportunities for catch-up and consolidation are built into the curriculum. The real gap, however, is likely to be a question of cultural capital. Pupils from disrupted backgrounds, with poor home lives, are much more likely to have missed out on the cultural education that middle-class children take for granted: access to books at home; stimulating adult conversation; trips to museums and theatres etc. High quality curriculum plans recognise this and build in opportunities for pupils to explore the background of the topics studied, and in implementing those plans, teachers are able to go some way towards filling in the cultural knowledge which some pupils lack.

15

What about differentiation?

Ofsted has a problem with differentiation. As Ofsted inspectors know, there are certain words to be avoided in inspection reports, and when the EIF was published, differentiation joined the banned list. In paragraph 26, we are told that inspectors will make a judgement on the quality of education by evaluating the extent to which:

> teachers present subject matter clearly, promoting appropriate discussion about the subject matter they are teaching. They check learners' understanding systematically, identify misconceptions accurately and provide clear, direct feedback. In doing so, they respond and adapt their teaching as necessary, without unnecessarily elaborate or differentiated approaches.[1]

The phrase 'without unnecessarily elaborate or differentiated approaches' is slipped in almost as an afterthought, and has caused immense confusion. If a teacher is expected to ensure that every child in the class makes progress, how can that be done without differentiating? Differentiation has long been fundamental to good classroom practice but suddenly it appeared to be deemed unnecessary.

Section 5 of *The Teachers' Standards* states that teachers 'must adapt teaching to respond to the strengths and needs of all pupils.' They must 'know when and how to differentiate appropriately, using approaches which enable pupils to be taught effectively.'[2] How then does this square with the Ofsted guidance?

Part of the problem lies in inspectors' reluctance to use the term. As inspectors struggled to discuss lessons without mentioning differentiation, teachers quickly picked up on their confusion and assumed that differentiation had become a somewhat dubious concept. In reality, inspectors of course consider differentiation, even if they have been trained to avoid the word itself. But why should this be so? The answer can be found in the word 'unnecessarily'. A key feature of the EIF is the focus on teacher workload and, as all new teachers know, attempting to differentiate material for thirty mixed ability pupils can become a never-ending task. Teachers can spend hours creating tailor made worksheets to accommodate pupil needs and, indeed, many do. Ofsted's guidance provides a sensible antidote to this approach. Teachers are now urged not to spend hours on 'unnecessarily elaborate or differentiated approaches' but they should nevertheless differentiate to ensure that every pupil in the class is able to make progress in their learning.

Of course, at the end of a teaching cycle, within a curriculum progress model, assessment should show exactly which goals have been met by each pupil. This does not mean, however, that teachers should go mad in attempting to ensure that there are never any gaps by attempting to provide differentiated materials for everyone in the class. There are less time consuming and more effective ways to achieve the same ends. A teacher who spends every night creating infinitely differentiated materials is unlikely to be effective in the classroom the next day – and half dead by the end of term. As in all things, a balanced approach is essential. Teachers need to think carefully about curriculum content and how it can be adapted to meet pupils' needs. They also need to be able to check on learning regularly to identify potential learning gaps so that they can modify the next few teaching episodes. They will still need to use differentiated materials where necessary, and to differentiate their delivery of the lesson as they move around the classroom, but they cannot be expected to prepare individually packaged lessons for every child in the class.

Differentiation has to be handled with care, however, and it is important to distinguish between differentiating in order to facilitate learning and differentiated learning outcomes. If teachers plan for different outcomes for the pupils in their classes, they effectively signal to students that a decision has been made that only a few can reach the top. If pupils see there is a choice regarding how much they need to learn in a lesson, then it is too tempting for them to coast along doing the bare minimum. Learning intentions are key here: teachers need to ensure that they communicate to all pupils the expectation that they should all be thinking deeply and pushing their learning.

Ofsted inspectors will continue to avoid using the word, but as they consider whether progress is being made in the lessons they visit, they will see effective teachers taking pains to help struggling pupils understand new learning as well as challenging those who grasp new ideas, skills and concepts quickly. They will also consider whether the teacher is aware of any gaps in learning and is doing something to address them. Middle leaders therefore need to reassure the teachers in their teams that differentiation is still important, even if Ofsted inspectors seem never to mention it.

Notes

1 *The Education Inspection Framework.* (2019). 190015. Crown Copyright 2019, p. 9.
2 *The Teachers' Standards.* (2011). DFE-00066-2011 https://www.gov.uk/government/publications/teachers-standards p.11.

16
From intent to implementation

Skilled middle leaders give a great deal of thought to the nature of their subjects and what they want pupils to learn. They are able to articulate their ideas clearly, refine them in consultation with their team members, and express them succinctly in up to date subject documentation. They have clear ideas about the shape of learning in each year group, and an understanding that the curriculum is much more than simply a series of steps towards public examinations or tests. Put simply, they are well prepared. The consideration of intent is vital to successful learning; implementation then becomes much more straightforward as it is founded upon solid principles and well thought out learning goals.

PART

2 IMPLEMENTATION

17

What is meant by implementation?

The *School Inspection Handbook* defines implementation as 'the way that the curriculum developed or adopted by the school is taught and assessed in order to support pupils to build their knowledge and to apply that knowledge as skills.'[1] It goes on to list what Ofsted inspectors, based on their research, regard as the most important factors in how, and how effectively, the curriculum is taught and assessed. The list focuses on what teachers should be doing in the classroom. They should:

- Have expert knowledge.
- Enable pupils to understand key concepts.
- Check pupils' understanding effectively.
- Ensure that pupils embed key concepts in their long-term memory.
- Use assessment to check pupils' understanding in order to inform teaching.

What follows is an attempt to elucidate and clarify this approach, but it goes beyond Ofsted's narrow definition of implementation in order to cover all aspects of the subject, including the practical questions middle leaders need to consider in order to run successful departments or subject teams. Curriculum implementation, teachers' subject knowledge, and assessment are all considered in depth but, in order to ensure that the role of the middle leader in implementing his or her vision for the subject is covered comprehensively, a wide range of more practical issues is considered. So, in addition to the areas suggested by Ofsted, the topics covered range from closing the gap to the importance of seating plans, from the nature of questioning to what to look for in books, from the importance of literacy to how to deal with underperformance. Attention is also paid to the mundane but vital activities which comprise a necessary, if unexciting, element of the middle leader's role: team meetings, dealing with examination boards, data analysis, etc.

Note

1 *The School Inspection Handbook* (September 2019). 190017. Crown Copyright 2019, p. 41.

18

How important is subject knowledge?

There are two issues here: teachers' subject knowledge and the subject knowledge pupils need to make progress in their learning.

The *School Inspection Handbook* makes it clear that teachers should have a good knowledge of the subjects they teach. It insists that:

> Teachers have expert knowledge of the subjects that they teach. If they do not, they are supported to address gaps in their knowledge so that pupils are not disadvantaged by ineffective teaching.[1]

Parents and, indeed, pupils, expect teachers to be subject experts. The term 'expert' might perhaps be a little optimistic, but it is not unreasonable to expect teachers to be good at the subjects they teach. This does not mean they should all be educated to Ph.D. standard, but they should have a comprehensive knowledge of what they are teaching. There is nothing more dispiriting when observing lessons to see teachers who don't have a firm grasp of their subjects. A factual error may be quickly passed over, but it is important to remember that thirty children may have absorbed that fact and assumed, because they trust their teachers, it is accurate. Senior and middle leaders often turn a blind eye to the odd mistake, particularly if it is a spelling or punctuation error, but they should never do so.

Of course, teachers make mistakes, but they must be aware of the impact of those mistakes on the pupils they teach. If they are unaware that they are making mistakes, they need to be told so that they can correct them. I have seen too many lessons where teachers confuse 'its' and 'it's', for example. This is one of those common errors which are often disregarded simply because they are common errors, but these things matter. Teachers who regularly make such simple mistakes convince pupils that they don't really matter. When headteachers make such mistakes – and some do – and then create publicity materials with spelling or punctuation errors which they proudly display outside the school, they not only send a message to the community that the school doesn't pay attention to detail, but also they undermine confidence in the teaching profession in general. It is up to both senior and middle leaders, therefore, to ensure that teachers have the knowledge they need to maintain an appropriate level of expertise. This may involve some difficult conversations, especially if the teacher disregards concern about what many consider to be minor factual or grammatical errors, but if standards are to be maintained they are essential. If teachers want to be regarded as professionals, pride in their subject knowledge is essential. Perhaps the term 'expert' is not optimistic after all.

Subject knowledge is not simply a matter of knowing the facts, of course. In its summary of the research underpinning the new framework, Ofsted offers an interesting definition of subject knowledge:

> If curriculum lies at the heart of education, and subject lies at the heart of curriculum, then it follows that teachers need solid knowledge and under-standing of the subject(s) they teach. As well as this, they need to know how to teach that subject, and, more generally, how to teach. These three types of essential knowledge are known as content knowledge, pedagogical knowl-edge and pedagogical content knowledge. Content knowledge can be defined as teachers' knowledge of the subject they are teaching, pedagogical knowl-edge as teachers' knowledge of effective teaching methods, and pedagogical content knowledge as teachers' knowledge of how to teach the particular sub-ject or topic.[2]

Parents and pupils are likely to focus on content knowledge when considering teachers' credibility, but senior and middle leaders will also need to assure them-selves that their colleagues have a good understanding of appropriate general teaching methods as well as subject-specific pedagogical techniques. Teachers therefore require a sophisticated understanding of both their subject and class-room pedagogy. Ofsted's research paper offers an outline of the knowledge needed by Early Years teachers to illustrate this point:

> Early years educators need a wide range of specific knowledge, including on children's physical and mental development, communication, and learning and teaching in specific subjects and areas of development. To teach early mathematics effectively, educators need to know how children develop math-ematical understanding and how to assess this development. They need to know how children develop language and literacy, and how to teach early phonics. The types of knowledge early years teachers need are therefore simi-lar too, but also distinct from those of teachers in the later years of primary and beyond. Like other teachers, they require subject knowledge and peda-gogical knowledge (though the latter of course here refers to early years peda-gogy), but there is a greater stress on knowledge of learners, learning and child development, due to the rapid development of children at this age, and on communication. Teachers need to know how children develop and learn and have a clear understanding of possible next steps in their development and learning.[3]

Early years teachers are something of a special case because they need a much broader knowledge base than those who teach older children, but the point here is that knowledge is a complex concept which demands close attention. Successful teaching is a sophisticated activity.

In the current educational climate, we must, of course, acknowledge that not all classes will be taught by subject specialists. The combination of chronic underfunding and the lack of high quality graduates entering the profession has led to severe shortages. This means that some subjects have to be taught by teachers who do not really have the expertise to do so. This has been a problem in maths, in particular, for some time, but it is now becoming an issue in virtually every area of the curriculum. These teachers need careful support. Some opt for re-training, but many find themselves suddenly expected to teach subjects about which they have little knowledge. It then becomes the responsibility of middle leaders to ensure that they have sufficient subject knowledge, and a good understanding of essential subject-specific pedagogy, to teach effectively. This means intensive CPD, intensive support, and frequent lesson monitoring. Ofsted describes this simply as providing support in addressing gaps in their knowledge but, in practice, this is major task.

Now let's turn to the pupils and the subject knowledge and skills they need to achieve success. Disciplinary knowledge is, of course, fundamental to understanding, but thought needs to be given both to the nature of that knowledge and how much knowledge is needed. We have already considered the importance of selection and sequencing in curriculum planning but there is also the simple question of quantity. The exact amount of knowledge necessary will differ by age group and level taught, and teachers need to think carefully about whether pupils have the knowledge they need both to understand the subject and make appropriate progress. Too much knowledge may well limit attainment. Pupils who are presented with huge amounts of information can easily become overloaded, and their learning slows as a result. On the other hand, if teachers impart insufficient knowledge, their understanding of the subject will suffer, and future learning may become too difficult.

Finally, teachers also need to think about the way knowledge is acquired by young people in the digital age. When facts can be checked almost instantly on laptops, tablets and mobile phones, learning facts strikes them as pointless and unnecessary. Why do I need to commit a series of dates or chemical formulae to memory, when I can look them up wherever I find myself? The easy answer, and the one most teachers find themselves using, is that you won't be able to look things up in the examination room, but it is also important to explain that the acquisition of knowledge depends on prior learning. If pupils do not have a firm foundation of knowledge, subsequent learning becomes almost impossible.

At first glance, there is a certain irony in the fact that the acquisition of knowledge in a landscape dominated by Google is becoming increasingly important in contemporary pedagogy, but the very fact that information is now so easily accessible has served to highlight the importance of knowledge in developing understanding. Put simply, pupils need to learn things to be able to learn more. If they can't remember what they have learnt, future learning becomes much more difficult. Google may offer an unbelievably comprehensive compendium of information, but it can't replace memory. If pupils remember more, they learn more.

Notes

1 *Ibid. p.44*
2 *Education Inspection Framework: Overview of Research.* (2019). 180045. Crown Copyright 2019. p.9.
3 Ibid. p.11.

19
Are knowledge organisers the answer?

In seeking to ensure that pupils in their classes have the knowledge they need, teachers are increasingly turning to subject organisers, but how useful are they? They may well turn out to be little more than a fad, but many educationalists regard them as important aids to learning and their ubiquity suggests that they may be genuinely effective in promoting success. They take many different forms, but most cover a single sheet of A4 and include an outline of the topic being studied, a list of key words, important equations, key learning points etc. They tend not to show pupils how to learn – that's the teacher's job – but focus instead on simple terms of what to learn.

Knowledge organisers have many benefits for hard pressed teachers. They are useful for curriculum planning – they are in some respects mini-curriculum plans in themselves – and, if employed judiciously, they can be used regularly in lessons and in the setting of homework tasks. It has to be acknowledged, of course, that their popularity is partly due to the fact that they seem to offer an easy way of demonstrating curriculum intent to inspectors. They also enable teachers to ensure that gaps in learning are filled. Pupils who miss lessons can be directed towards key sections of their organisers, for example. Used correctly, they can be a valuable inclusion tool, enabling pupils to consolidate their learning outside of the classroom, perhaps working with a teaching assistant or a specialist teacher.

Teaching assistants find knowledge organisers particularly useful as they give a clear idea of the key learning points to be covered by the pupils in their care. One of the biggest weaknesses in the classroom is the failure of teachers to make good use of teaching assistants, usually because they don't have the time to brief them properly on the plans for their lessons and the support particular pupils might need. This means that far too often teaching assistants stand around doing very little. Knowledge organisers are able provide the guidance they need to offer much more useful, targeted support.

There are strong benefits for pupils too. They can see the bigger picture straightaway and they are able to see the direction of their learning from the outset. They are also able to look back on what they have learnt to check they can still remember it, and they can gain confidence from having key knowledge readily accessible whenever it is needed. Pupils are also encouraged to gain a greater sense of responsibility for their own learning as they consult their organisers whenever they feel they need to. A knowledge organiser is therefore what once would have been called a *vade mecum*, a handbook or guide constantly on hand for consultation.

Used regularly in the classroom, knowledge organisers can contribute to lessons in many ways. Key facts can be learnt prior to the lesson thus obviating the need to spend valuable time on them in class, and less able pupils are able to take more time without feeling embarrassed in front of their peers. In this sense, knowledge organisers offer a simple means of pre-teaching which can help lessons get started quickly and progress more rapidly. They are also useful if the learning is spaced out, or, as discussed earlier, interleaved because pupils are able quickly to recall previous learning without the need for long and involved revision sessions in class. The ability to look back on learning in this way reinforces retrieval skills thus making it more likely that pupils will remember more.

All this seems to suggest that knowledge organisers are invaluable teaching tools which all teachers should be using. They do, however, have their weaknesses. A recent exchange I had in a primary classroom makes the point neatly. I asked a pupil to show me her knowledge organiser and asked how she used it. After a few minutes of shuffling through her exercise book, and her folder containing her best work, she dragged out a scruffy sheet of A4 and explained that the teacher had given it to her at the beginning of the year. I asked if she knew what she had to do with it and she immediately replied, 'Stick it in the front of my book', looking worried because she clearly hadn't done so. For her, it was simply another piece of paper, forgotten and filed away. If knowledge organisers are to be of any use, they must be used regularly, and pupils need to be taught how to use them. Teachers, too, need to be convinced of their use. I suspect that in schools across the country, subject teams have got together to create impressive documents which are forgotten about a few weeks later as they fall back on familiar classroom activities.

There is also a danger that pupils come to regard the content of their knowledge organisers as the sum total of all they need to learn. If they quickly absorb the key information set out in front of them, they can doze quietly through lessons without really putting themselves out. Success is assured because everything they need to know has been captured on one marvellous sheet of A4.

Another problem relates to design. Choosing what is included in a knowledge organiser is a difficult task. The activity itself is useful for teachers to support their curriculum planning but it is easy to miss out key information which pupils subsequently need to further their learning. This often means that, in the pursuit of comprehensive coverage, one side of A4 becomes two or three, or something even more. Cleverly designed commercial knowledge organisers are now available but these are one-size-fits-all products which negate many of the advantages outlined above – in particular, teachers' involvement in curriculum planning.

If used carefully and regularly, knowledge organisers are valuable tools. However, they need to be thoughtfully designed and teachers need adequate training to ensure that they know how to use them effectively. Similarly, pupils need to be taught how to use them and to understand that they form only part of the learning process.

20

How should pupils be assessed?

Middle leaders are likely to spend a huge amount of time dealing with assessment and it can become one of the most frustrating and worrying aspects of the job. Part of the problem stems from confusion over terminology: assessment can be too closely linked to attainment; it is often confused with marking; teachers are often unclear what is meant by feedback; and the line between formative and summative assessment is often hard to define. There is also the additional issue of teacher workload, particularly in schools with complex monitoring systems which demand frequent data drops.

The first step is to ensure that everyone in the department is clear about the difference between formative and summative assessment. The aim of formative assessment is to inform the teacher about the performance, skills and knowledge of pupils in his or her classes so that learning can be planned, misunderstandings corrected, and misconceptions identified. It is essentially a check on learning. Following a formative assessment, it is up to teachers to put things in place to ensure that pupils continue learning. They might offer feedback, either to individuals or to the class as a whole, they might decide to revise a particular topic, they might introduce a range of tasks designed to revisit the skills and knowledge which has not been fully understood. The ultimate aim is to promote learning. If nothing is done as a result of an assessment, then it loses its value.

Summative assessment, as the term implies, sums up what has been learnt so far. It is essentially a quality control method which provides a snapshot of how a pupil, or group of pupils, has performed over a set period of time. An end of term test which leads simply to a grade on a report is the obvious example. Of course, some forms of assessment can be both summative and formative, provided the teacher uses feedback to advance the learning once the test has been administered.

Formative assessment is key to successful learning and it is the type of assessment to which middle leaders should devote the most time. It will be successful only if pupils understand its purpose and how it works, and teachers ensure that enough time is given to allow pupils to respond appropriately.

Feedback, for example, need not be too long or too involved. Indeed, too much feedback is more likely to confuse than elucidate. Activities stemming from formative assessment should be carefully targeted, focusing initially on one or two learning points to which pupils are able to respond. There should be opportunities built in which encourage revision or another attempt at a task to help secure the learning. It should not, however, become too routine. In some classes I have observed, a ten-minute period is set aside every lesson for pupils to respond to the feedback the teacher has given on their homework, and while this should be a useful opportunity for further learning, it is clear that most of the class were writing perfunctory responses without really thinking about them. They were passing the time until the lesson proper began.

Peer assessment is becoming increasingly popular, and this too can be a powerful learning tool, but pupils need to be taught how to do it. Feedback that takes the form of simplistic comments such as 'very good writing' or 'this would be better if you had used more description' are pointless and simply waste time. If pupils are trained to look for specifics, however, they can advance both the learning of their partner and their own learning. Nor should whole class feedback be dismissed as too impersonal. If a teacher has read thirty essays many of which make the same error, or demonstrate a similar misconception, then there is no reason why the feedback cannot be directed towards the whole class. The important point, of course, is that the feedback should not take the form of the teacher simply telling the class where everyone went wrong – the class should be encouraged to respond in some way so that the learning sinks in.

Perhaps the most effective formative assessment is self-assessment. If the learning culture is strong enough, and the pupil really wants to learn, then he or she is likely to be highly critical. This means that work will be scrutinised closely and checked carefully to ensure that is both accurate and of a high quality. Of course, teacher support will be necessary but truly switched on learners can make a huge amount of progress thanks largely due to their own efforts. How do pupils in underperforming schools taught by unskilled supply teachers end up with A* grades? They want to learn, and know how to learn. They become adept at setting personal goals and checking their learning.

Guiding the teachers in their departments or subject areas towards the use of effective formative assessment is one of the most important aspects of the middle leader's role. Regular and carefully planned CPD is essential but there is a major hurdle that has to be overcome first: too many teachers confuse formative assessment with marking. This is partly due to what can be described as not only an historical marking culture in the profession, but also a result of parental pressure. Put simply, parents expect to see books marked, and lots of teachers still don't feel that they are doing a proper job if their pupils' work is not regularly covered in red ink. Good marking is often seen as a proxy for good teaching but there is lots of evidence to suggest that this is simply not the case. It is important, therefore, for middle leaders to be clear about the distinction between marking and assessment, and to make their expectations clear regarding the nature of the formative assessment expected in their classrooms. A strong assessment policy is always a feature of good subject departments. It will, of course, have to align with whole school policies – and these need to be communicated and justified to parents – but it is in its implementation in the classroom where its effectiveness will be revealed.

Formative assessment techniques should be regularly discussed in department and subject team meetings so that best practice can be shared, and approaches standardised. Devising tasks which lead to real improvements in learning can be difficult, so the greater the sharing, the more effective the tasks are likely to be. It is particularly important for new and inexperienced staff to discuss such issues and their use of assessment should form a key strand in any coaching or induction programmes offered by the school.

Summative assessment is much more straightforward, but it is not without its issues. This type of assessment is there to measure and record progress, and since the introduction of performance tables it has become more and more dominant in schools. In some cases, teachers have been overwhelmed by senior leaders' expectations regarding assessment. The workload agreement was helpful in suggesting a limit to the number of 'data drops' per year, especially since some leadership teams were demanding half-termly, monthly or even weekly input from teachers, but the need to provide accurate information can still be something of a burden, particularly for heads of department.

Three data drops a year seems reasonable and allows teachers and leaders to check on progress at the end of every term. However, the data needs to be accurate and it here that middle leaders often run into difficulties. With six data drops a year, teachers ended up simply inputting numbers into whatever software system the school employed just to get the task done and to satisfy the demands of senior leaders. The result was inaccurate and often fairly useless data. The conclusions drawn by the data analysts were often wildly inaccurate and sometimes led to unnecessary or even positively harmful interventions. With three data drops a year, it is much easier to produce useful data, but it is up to middle leaders to ensure its reliability.

Data must be accurate to be of any use. This means that grades or scores given by a teacher in one classroom must be in line with those in the classroom next door. This is not as easy to achieve as it sounds. Each teacher has to develop a good understanding of the criteria used for each grade, level or number, and their judgements have to be checked to ensure reliability. Moderation is therefore essential, and it is up to middle leaders to ensure that their colleagues are assessing accurately in line with departmental policies. In classes leading up to public examinations, moderation will be supported by examining boards, but it is equally important to ensure that standards are monitored in non-examination years to ensure that pupils are making appropriate progress. Lax monitoring can lead to pupils in one class falling well behind the others in the year group. Monitoring the quality of moderation is therefore ultimately about ensuring that the pace of learning is sustained across the department so that all pupils make the progress they should.

Highly effective middle leaders spend a lot of time ensuring that formative assessment is regularly discussed and carefully implemented; they also ensure that judgements are monitored, and standards maintained. Effective assessment is a skilled undertaking.

21

How do I fill gaps in pupils' learning?

The use of the phrase 'gaps in learning' has recently become ubiquitous in educational literature where it is sometimes confused with 'the learning gap' or 'closing the gap'. When we talk about gaps in learning we are referring to the learning missed in class, the learning missed as the curriculum is delivered. The phrase 'closing the gap' refers specifically to the gap between disadvantaged pupils and non-disadvantaged pupils and is considered below.

Good teaching has always sought to ensure that there are no gaps in a pupil's learning, but the new Ofsted framework has brought the issue to the fore. Consequently, teachers are now anxiously considering ways to ensure that gaps are filled and that no pupils are left behind. This is easy to say, but as with most aspects of education, harder to do in practice. There are, of course, many reasons why a pupil might fall behind in his or her learning. High levels of absence have a significant impact on learning, whether through illness, family holidays or truancy. An inability to cope with the pace of learning is another factor: a student who doesn't grasp a skill or concept as quickly as others in the class will fall behind – and fall further behind as his or her lack of knowledge snowballs. Then there is the relentless pressure teachers feel to move on. In an overcrowded curriculum, teachers are acutely conscious of the need to begin the next unit of work despite the fact that there are students in the class who are clearly struggling to keep up. There are also the disaffected students to consider – the ones who don't want to be there and the ones with better things to do. Poor behaviour may also be a contributing factor here, especially if behaviour is bad enough to disrupt the learning in class.

A tired teacher looking out at 30 pupils, some of whom are often absent, a few who have just come back from holidays, several who are simply not interested, and some who just can't keep up despite their enthusiasm for the subject, may well regard filling gaps as next to impossible. It is probably fair to say that not too many years ago this was an issue which most teachers quietly ignored. They knew that pupils were falling behind and felt that nothing could be done about it – they had deadlines to meet, content to deliver, and examinations to prepare for. They simply pushed on regardless. Thankfully, this attitude is no longer tolerated, and teachers now have to think carefully about filling as many gaps as possible. There isn't a perfect solution but there is a lot that can be done to help most pupils towards a more comprehensive understanding of the curriculum.

First and foremost, we return to the question of culture. As we have seen, if a strong learning culture has been established in the school and in the subject, pupils are much more likely to be anxious to fill the gaps themselves. If they are fully engaged, and really enjoy their learning, they will want to catch up with anything they have missed. The most conscientious will do this by asking their teacher or talking with their friends; others may need gentle prompting but make the effort once they have been asked to do so.

A key part of a strong learning culture requires teachers to be consistent and, indeed, relentless. Pupils know which teachers will press them for homework and which ones will quietly forget if the homework is not forthcoming; they know who will insist that missing notes are copied up and who won't bother. Teachers who are relentless in their pursuit of missing work quickly find that the majority of pupils catch up. Once their expectations have been established, pupils tend to fulfil them. Pupils tend, in their own approach to lessons, to mirror the teacher's approach. If he or she is rigorous and expects work to be done on time, it generally is; if a teacher is lax and careless, then pupils quickly pick up on this and respond accordingly. The relentless approach is initially very time-consuming as pupils have to be chased again and again. This is not simply a matter of reminding them to complete work once or twice, but often entails seeking them out around the school, keeping them in detention, sending letters home etc. However, once the teacher has established a reputation for relentlessness, pupils respond and the workload diminishes. There will always be pupils who don't complete the work no matter how relentlessly they are pursued, but if the learning culture is established securely, most will.

In order to ensure that gaps can be filled, the curriculum needs to be carefully planned. We have already considered the importance of interleaving and spaced learning, but there should always be an element of circularity built into any subject curriculum. This doesn't mean unnecessary repetition, but it does mean that learning should be kept alive throughout the course. Topics should not be taught and forgotten until the end of the year tests, they should be linked together so that prior learning is drawn upon again and again. A well-planned curriculum makes this possible.

There is also a range of teaching techniques which help to secure learning and help pupils remember more. The most obvious is, of course, individual support. Teachers are good at helping individuals. If they recognise that a pupil doesn't understand and is falling behind, they are able to provide support in the lesson or help them to catch up after school. Teaching assistants are invaluable in this regard and are often able to spend time with pupils to ensure that any work missed is covered and gaps are quickly filled. This does, of course, rely on the school having sufficient funding to employ enough staff to make this possible. It also requires strong observational and diagnostic skills on the part of the teacher, as well as a preparedness to intervene and support where necessary. As most schools realise, individual support is a powerful tool and most schools now offer a range of after school or lunch time catch-up sessions for pupils who have fallen behind. Commercial tutoring companies have long recognised the power of individual support and thrive on promoting its importance and effectiveness.

Teachers are now beginning to spend more time in lessons recalling prior learning. Warm up exercises or 'now tasks' are often used at the start of lessons to remind pupils of what they learnt in previous lessons, and many now encourage recall of skills and knowledge acquired much earlier in the course. Quizzes and quick-fire tests are becoming more and more popular and for good reasons. They provide a strong start to the lesson and, best of all, pupils enjoy them. They like the competitive atmosphere and they enjoy showing off what they know. The key point, of course, is that students are given opportunities to revisit past content and to refine their understandings of old material.

It is important too, when planning lessons, to ensure that gaps are not created almost by accident. This can happen if new learning is introduced too quickly or not carefully enough. It may be necessary, therefore, to recognise that new content sometimes needs to be modified so that it is approachable for all students, especially those with a weaker knowledge of previous material. Students will have an easier time learning new content if it is not assumed that all of them have a complete understanding what has gone on before. So, when presenting new material consider using some basic skills and knowledge to help ease the way into more difficult areas. For example, a maths teacher might consider using easier numbers, fewer fractions, and generally more straightforward problems as the starting point. This way, struggling students can begin to grasp the important ideas of the new material without being handicapped by their fragile understanding of the old.

For middle leaders, the challenge is once again to ensure consistency across the subject or department. Teachers need to be trained in the most effective 'gap filling' techniques, and common approaches to quizzing or 'now tasks' need to be created and shared. Careful monitoring of the quality of teaching is also be needed to ensure that teachers are relentless in their approach to missing work and consider catch-up activities as essential. It is also important to co-ordinate the work of teaching assistants and to deliver the training necessary to help them identify gaps and provide the necessary one-to-one support some pupils will undoubtedly need.

22
How do I close the gap?

The gap between the progress and attainment of disadvantaged pupils and their non-disadvantaged peers is something of a national scandal. Disadvantaged pupils start school already behind their peers and the gap grows as they move up through the system. Indeed, it has been estimated that disadvantaged pupils fall behind their more affluent peers by around two months each year over the course of secondary school.[1] Undoubtedly, inequities in the structure of the education system in the UK exacerbate the problem as it is a system designed primarily for the middle and upper classes. With independent and highly selective grammar schools – where most of the decision makers send their children – regarded as the acme of a good education, it is not surprising that state schools sometimes struggle to offer the quality of education needed to ensure that all pupils make the same degree of progress.

There is evidence, however, that, until the arrival of Covid-19, the gap was beginning to close. According to the Education Policy Institute, over the past decade the attainment gap between disadvantaged pupils and their classmates at the end of primary school is estimated to have narrowed from 11.5 months to 9.2 months in 2019.[2] It is difficult to measure the impact of extended periods of school closures on disadvantaged pupils, but it is obvious they will have suffered. Unlike their more affluent peers, they may not have been able to access the online learning provided by most schools, they may have found it impossible to work in overcrowded accommodation, they may have had limited access to books and other resources, and their parents may not have had the time or the cultural capital to guide them in their learning. In an analysis of the issue in May 2020, the Education Endowment Foundation expressed fears that the progress made since 2011 will be lost almost completely.[3] Consequently, there is now an even more pressing need to improve the life chances of disadvantaged pupils.

Recently more attention has been paid to the issue of cultural capital, which Sean Harford described as '…the essential knowledge that pupils need to be educated citizens, introducing them to the best that has been thought and said, and helping to engender an appreciation of human creativity and achievement.'[4]

The problem, of course, is that many children grow up in homes where there are limited opportunities for the transmission of cultural capital. They grow up without books, without access to the internet, without the chance to experience cultural activities like theatre and museum visits that most children take for granted. Above all, they grow up in households where they simply hear fewer words.

The now famous American study by Hart and Risley, which came to be known as 'the word gap', provides a good illustration of just how difficult this process of catching up really is. In their book *Meaningful Differences in the Everyday Experience of Young American Children*,[5] they recorded hundreds of hours of language used by children in different households over a two-and-a-half-year period. Families were classified by their socio-economic status. Their findings were quite shocking: they discovered that in four years, an average child in a professional family experienced almost 45 million words, an average child in a working-class family 26 million words, and an average child in a family on welfare 13 million words. Put simply, a child from a disadvantaged background enters the education system 30 million words behind children who have grown up in professional homes.

Children learn so much in the first few years of their lives that it is not surprising that catching up later becomes incredibly difficult for them, as well as for the teachers trying to overcome years of neglect. Middle leaders confronted by the need to explain to senior leaders and governors why the gap between disadvantaged pupils and their more privileged peers in their departments is so wide would do well to remember that they are effectively trying to correct years of missed learning. Nevertheless, even if it feels like King Canute trying to hold back the tide, the attempt must, of course, be made.

The first step is to ensure that everyone in the department knows who the disadvantaged pupils are. This may sound obvious, but I have been in far too many classrooms where the teachers have no idea about this at all. Others rely too heavily on class lists. They know that they have a list with the pupil premium recipients clearly marked but they rarely consult it. Once they know who these pupils are, they are in a position to support them. Some hide behind the notion that whole class teaching is the answer, but this doesn't mean they don't have to know who their pupils are. High quality teaching is of course fundamental to securing the progress of everyone in the room, but it doesn't mean that individual differences can be ignored. Conscientious middle leaders make a point of regularly dropping into classrooms to check on the progress of disadvantaged pupils, thus ensuring that their staff know who they are and think about the support they need on a day to day basis.

Of course, disadvantaged doesn't necessarily mean low ability. It is important therefore to ensure that high expectations are maintained for all pupils in the class, whatever their backgrounds. Teachers should never be allowed to get away with saying things like, 'What chance does she stand with a family like that? Her brother was just the same.' This means that the progress of disadvantaged pupils needs to be regularly scrutinised to ensure that they are keeping pace with their peers. The relentless approach to gap filling described above is key here.

Many disadvantaged pupils will have gaps in their learning, and these have to diagnosed. Tests on entry to the school provide a certain amount of information but it is in class where the gaps become obvious. Teachers must therefore be alert to situations where pupils are clearly struggling simply because they have not had the learning experiences of their peers. Simple factual gaps can easily be filled; others may take longer.

Good schools have long been aware of the importance of cultural capital and offer a wide range of trips, visits, after school clubs, visiting speakers etc. to make sure that all their pupils gain a rich cultural experience. Middle leaders need to think carefully about the subject-specific gaps they may need to fill. There are obvious examples: the English department will want to make sure that pupils studying drama get the chance to see a play performed by a professional theatre company; the music department will want to offer pupils opportunities to hear live music in range of genres; and language teachers will be keen to give pupils the chance to travel abroad. Pupil premium funding makes events like this possible, but it is up to middle leaders to make them happen.

High performing subject departments now offer comprehensive packages to support disadvantaged children. They ensure that teachers know their pupils and are alert to potential gaps in learning; they provide one-to-one support as necessary; they offer lunchtime and after school catch-up sessions; they meet regularly with parents; and they seek out cultural experiences to enrich their learning. They maintain high expectations and they rarely give up on even the most difficult to reach students. At the end of the year they may have closed the gap by only a few points but that is a significant achievement in itself.

Notes

1 Andrews, J, Robinson D, Hutchinson J. (2017). *Closing the Gap? Trends in Educational Disadvantage*. Education Policy Institute. 2017. p.6. https://epi.org.uk/wp-content/uploads/2017/08/Closing-the-Gap_EPI-.pdf

2 Education Policy Institute. *Education in England Annual Report 2019*. https://epi.org.uk/wp-content/uploads/2019/07/EPI-Annual-Report-2019.pdf

3 Education Endowment Foundation. (2020). *Rapid Evidence Assessment: Impact of school closures on the attainment gap*. https://educationendowmentfoundation.org.uk/public/files/REA_-_Impact_of_school_closures_on_the_attainment_gap_summary.pdf

4 Harford, S. (2019). *School Inspection Update – January 2019 Special Edition* 180119. Crown Copyright 2019. www.gov.uk/government/organisations/ofsted. p.10.

5 *B. Hart & T. Risley. (1995). Meaningful Differences in the Everyday Experience of Young American Children. P.H. Brookes.*

23

What is really meant by 'challenge'?

Few would disagree that pupils need to be challenged if they are to make good progress in their learning but the word itself has become something of a *bête noire* in the classroom as teachers struggle to understand exactly what it means and how to do it. It is not simply a question of setting difficult work or making sure that extension tasks are readily available; it is more of a mindset – an approach to learning which ensures that everyone in the class is aiming for the top.

As we saw in the section on differentiation, it is important to ensure that teachers do not plan for differentiated outcomes. If they do this, some pupils may well assume that they cannot get very far in their learning and do as little as possible as a result. The teacher needs to make clear his or her learning intentions so that everyone in the class is aware that no limits have been set on their learning and they are all expected to work as hard as they can. Again, we come back to the importance of a strong learning culture where pupils are keen to learn and ready to stretch themselves. They should be aiming to master a subject rather than achieve the more obvious goals such as examination grades or the approbation of their teachers and peers. The term 'mastery' has to be handled with care – it is now overused in schools, and often widely misunderstood, thanks largely to attempts to translate the concept of mathematical mastery promoted by Maths Hubs to other subjects – but its original meaning is key to the notion of challenge. In *Visible Learning for Teachers*, John Hattie describes three types of learning goals:

- *Mastery* – students aim to develop their competence and consider ability to be developed by increasing effort.

- *Performance* – students aim to outperform their peers. They consider ability to be fixed, not able to be changed.

- *Social* – students are concerned about how they relate to others.[1]

In classrooms where there is real challenge, pupils understand that there is no limit to what they can learn provided they apply sufficient effort.

For some teachers, the answer to successful challenge lies in independence. Once pupils have developed a degree of independence, and if they are lucky enough to be supported by a strong learning culture, they will take charge of their own learning and begin to challenge themselves. Pupils who behave in this way will undoubtedly make good progress in their learning – and sometimes amazing progress – but not all of them will. Independence needs to be encouraged but also nurtured. Sometimes, independence ends up limiting learning. Teachers sometimes forget that pupils need to possess a significant amount of knowledge before they are ready to work independently. There is no real challenge posed if a pupil is told to go off and be independent if, once they get there, they don't have the knowledge or skills to complete the task successfully. Most middle leaders will be familiar with independent learning projects set by teachers as challenge tasks which end up with page after page of beautifully presented information but virtually no evidence of learning.

Successful independent learning is dependent upon pupils having a high degree of motivation plus the necessary knowledge both to complete the task and go beyond it if possible. Much depends upon the approach taken by the teacher, however. Hattie talks about teachers as 'activators' and 'evaluators.' An activator is

> … any agency bringing about change, or something that 'increases the activity of an enzyme or a protein that increases the production of a gene product in DNA transcription'. This notion has action, agency, and augmentation – and thus is a most appropriate metaphor for describing the major role of the teacher.[2]

He describes the role of 'evaluator' as one in which the teacher is able to consider 'the worth and merit of the activation.' This means worth and merit for its own sake, and not with the narrow aim of considering its worth in relation to examination outcomes. Highly effective teachers are able to combine the two roles in order to focus more closely on the quality of the learning, and the impact they are having on all pupils, rather than their rate of progress through the curriculum or examination results.

However bright and self-motivated, pupils need clear goals if they are going to work independently, with carefully considered steps to success so that they can judge how well they are working towards those goals. To do this, they need to be taught to think in specific ways so that, when they face difficulties, they can draw upon subject-specific strategies and questions to ask themselves to help them select the right knowledge to complete a task.

Challenge, of course, applies to all pupils and not just the brightest. It is therefore important to ensure that pupils are supported when they are challenged. If no limit is set on learning, and the bar is therefore set high, it is important to realise that individual pupil needs will have to be considered. Teachers must think about how a task is scaffolded and carefully select resources so all pupils can access the most challenging work. This might mean showing them high quality examples or providing literacy support. They could be directed towards their knowledge organisers if these are suitable. The support of their peers is another powerful resource – group work can be particularly challenging if the task is well thought out – and the value of extended periods of discussion should never be overlooked. I have observed too many lessons where discussions were shut down according to an arbitrary time limit when it was obvious that pupils were deeply involved in their learning. Nervous teachers who become anxious when being observed tend to think that they need to show that they are teaching and thus get worried if discussions go on too long. In the best lessons, however, teachers recognise that pupils are learning and let them continue to deepen their knowledge. The ability to judge when a discussion is coming to a natural close is a particular skill and reminds us of the importance Hattie's 'evaluators.'

High expectations on the part of the teacher are also evident in other ways. In order to 'soften the blow' of difficult material, teachers often fall back on simple language. They avoid academic vocabulary because they think it will confuse or get in the way of the learning. The opposite is true: children love learning new words and thy delight in showing off their knowledge of technical language. It gives them a sense of achievement and inspires confidence; consequently, they see 'difficult' learning as more worthwhile. Similarly, too many teachers simplify their feedback, commenting on simple errors rather than asking challenging questions or offering demanding follow-up tasks. As we shall see, the skilful use of questioning is also key to challenge. The ability to ask a challenging second question, or to push pupils on an answer they have given, is a powerful way of deepening learning.

Successful challenge in the classroom is a skilled activity. It involves high expectations, clear learning intentions, a focus on learning for the sake of learning, and a strong learning culture. It is not about extension activities or classes for the gifted and talented. It is for all pupils and not just the brightest, and it never sets limits on learning.

Notes

1 Hattie, J. *Visible Learning for Teachers: Maximising Impact on Learning.* (2012). Routledge. Taylor and Francis. Oxon., p. 43
2 Ibid. p.86.

24

What does good teaching look like in a lesson?

This is one of those questions which it may be impossible to answer definitively, but which every middle leader must address on a regular basis. There is little point in observing lessons if what you are looking for isn't clear. It is important for leaders at all levels to have a shared understanding of good teaching and this means that teaching is something which should be discussed at every opportunity. In schools where teaching and learning are the highest priorities – as they should be in all schools – what makes good teaching is regularly discussed at meetings of senior leaders, governors, staff and, above all, in subject team or department meetings. An effective middle leader will have his or her own ideas, but these need to be shared with the department and modified accordingly in order to generate consistency and common purpose. And since the perfect lesson will always be out of reach, leaders need to be open to new ideas and willing to update their views as part of their ongoing professional development. It should also go without saying that leaders should be good teachers themselves – and this, of course, includes headteachers.

In attempting to define a good lesson, it is customary to take lesson structure as the starting point. Most people would probably be content with a lesson outline which looks something like this:

- An initial overview of what the lesson will be about – its aims and objectives.

- Some kind of starter activity which gets the class ready to work, and draws on prior learning.

- An outline of the main ideas of the lesson.

- A series of varied activities designed to deliver the knowledge and skills required as effectively as possible.

- Regular checks on learning.

- A final activity which summarises the lesson, and checks that the key skills and ideas have been grasped.

■ A brief mention of what the next lesson will be about, so that pupils look forward to the next stage of their learning.

Teachers may want to include something about taking the class register and collecting homework, but most are likely to be happy with this basic outline. A good lesson is about more than a firm structure, however.

As we have seen, a strong learning culture is vital. Good teachers, therefore, must be able to engage pupils easily and inspire them in their learning. Judging how good they are at this is a skill in itself. We are all familiar with charismatic teachers who charm their classes into submission without really teaching much at all; we are also familiar with teachers whose technical skills are first-class but who bore pupils senseless. Experienced middle leaders look for a balanced approach and consider whether the enthusiasm the teacher engenders leads to real learning and whether the skilful delivery of the lesson is made sufficiently inspiring to fully engage pupils in their learning.

A strong learning culture can be recognised almost as soon as an observer walks into a room: pupils arrive on time, they settle quickly, they get their books out, they smile at the teacher, and they get straight down to the first task. As the lesson progresses it is clear that they are fully engaged in their learning: they behave well, they set about activities with enthusiasm, they ask questions, they take pride in their work, their books are well presented, and, at the end of the lesson, they are surprised at how quickly the time has gone.

Good teachers understand effective pedagogy and use a range of skills in their teaching. These include:

■ Careful planning.

■ Thorough knowledge of pupils as individuals.

■ Strong routines.

■ Clear presentation of ideas.

■ The ability to draw upon a comprehensive body of subject knowledge.

■ Effective questioning.

■ Varied activities including group and paired work.

■ The ability to adapt work to the needs of pupils.

■ Effective deployment of teaching assistants.

■ Preparedness to diverge from the lesson plan if it becomes clear that ideas have not been understood, and further practice is necessary to enable full understanding.

■ Regular checks on pupils' understanding.

- The ability to vary the pace of lessons according to the needs of the class.

- Good classroom control based upon engaging teaching rather than strict discipline.

I am sure there are many other skills which could be added to this list, but these are the kinds of things middle leaders should be looking for when judging the quality of teaching in their departments. It is important to remember, however, that teachers are human beings, and go about things in different ways. It is unreasonable to expect everyone to teach in exactly the same way, but it is not unreasonable to expect some degree of consistency. The real test, of course, is in terms of outcomes; not necessarily examination outcomes, although these are of course important, but outcomes in terms of pupil progress. What have pupils learnt at the end of the lesson?

This brings us to the pupils themselves. It is all too easy to judge good teaching solely according to teachers' views of what makes a good lesson. It is important, therefore, to ask pupils what they think. In my book, *The Gradual Art of School Improvement*, I described a series of activities I undertook as a headteacher aimed at understanding what pupils regarded as a good lesson. This involved discussions not only with the school council but with what I described as 'the alternative school council', a group of disaffected pupils chosen from each year group by their heads of year. They eventually came up with a fascinating list of things that they regarded as essential for a good lesson headed: *What makes good learning in a lesson at our school*[1]:

- Practising a new skill.

- Use of visual learning.

- Being encouraged to remember things your own way.

- Putting ideas/concepts in real world contexts.

- Students teaching each other, providing that everyone takes part and the class is under control.

- Teachers avoid lecturing but if they do pupils should be reminded to take notes.

- Positive, enthusiastic teachers and students.

- A comfortable atmosphere in class.

- Good relationships.

- Ensuring that everyone is involved throughout the lesson.

- No hands up.

- Non-embarrassing strategies for those who don't understand.

- Teachers fully aware of the range of ability in the class and providing for it.

- Teachers providing work to stretch the brightest and providing support for the weakest.

- A variety of activities helps but stopping and starting should be avoided, as should too much repetition.

- Regular revision should be a part of the lesson.

- The starter should be short and there should be a memorable summary at the end.

- Questioning should be used to check learning.

- Half-termly tests are useful to reinforce learning.

- Competition helps, especially among the brighter pupils.

- Homework should reinforce what has happened in the lesson or it should prepare for the next lesson.

- A reward system supports learning.

- Both students and teachers must be organised.

There is nothing earth shattering here, only a reminder of just how sharp pupils are when thinking about learning. After all, they have spent thousands of hours in the classroom and they know what works and what doesn't. It may be a little out of date now – a really useful exercise for middle leaders would be to update it in their own schools – but it does draw attention to some aspects of good teaching which teachers tend not to mention: the use of competition, for example, or the importance of avoiding embarrassment when pupils don't understand ideas straightaway.

There are, of course, additional criteria by which the quality of teaching may be judged. These include Ofsted guidance (although Ofsted firmly insists that it doesn't have a set formula for what a good lesson looks like, despite the fact that the 'Quality of Teaching' judgement is fairly specific at times), the advice of external consultants, more experienced colleagues, the views of senior leaders, and educational literature. These criteria need to be borne in mind and included in the overall picture of what a good lesson looks like, but they should not be allowed to dominate. An inexperienced middle leader may attempt to follow Ofsted guidance as closely as possible, for example, and thus end up with a fairly narrow definition of good teaching. It is important, therefore, for leaders to develop their own ideas based on all the evidence available and after a great deal of discussion at all levels both in and beyond school. Ultimately, however, whether a lesson is good or not is fairly obvious: most teachers recognise good teaching.

Note

1 Steward, R. *The Gradual Art of School Improvement.* (2019). London. Taylor and Francis. Oxon., p.143

25

How do I monitor the quality of teaching?

The quality of teaching has to be monitored nevertheless and this is an aspect of the role middle leaders often find difficult. They dislike the notion of observing their friends in the department, some of whom they will have been working along-side for years. It is easier with new colleagues and younger teachers, but a new head of department will find observing an older, more experienced colleague something of a challenge, especially if he or she is less than good. It has to be done, however, and there are very few schools nowadays where middle leaders do not regularly observe the colleagues in their departments or subject teams.

We must begin by distinguishing between observations which form part of the performance management process and those which form part of the day to day monitoring of teaching quality. Performance management observations generally follow a pattern dictated by senior leaders, usually with a set of whole school criteria. Though often stressful, they can be somewhat perfunctory, as those doing the observing normally have a good idea of what they are going to see, and those being observed are aware that something of a performance is expected. Of course, important decisions hang on such observations – threshold judgements, competence proceedings etc. – but the real monitoring of teaching quality generally takes place outside of these formal structures.

The question of culture is once again the key here. In departments where ideas are regularly shared and colleagues understand the importance of a collaborative approach to teaching, regular observations are simply part of day to day life. This does not mean the occasional drop-in, however; it means a fairly systemic approach to shared learning. The head of department who glibly says that he doesn't need to observe his colleagues teach because he is in and out of lessons all the time is missing the point. He may be able to see whether the class is engaged, behaving appropriately, and that the teacher is following the syllabus, but he won't get a real understanding of how the lesson develops, how the teacher checks on learning, and how he or she adapts the learning to the needs of the class. The best way of describing the necessary process is formal observation in an informal manner.

Middle leaders need to be able to create an environment in which teachers regularly spend time in each other's classrooms to enable them to share ideas, discuss lessons and improve their teaching. Observing lessons is thus about improving the teaching of both the observer and the observed: both colleagues are happy to share ideas, question and challenge one another, and both aim to improve. In this kind of environment, middle leaders will be able to observe lessons as part of the sharing process. Judgements will be made, of course, but they will be linked to discussions around improvement. As we have seen, the aim of good teaching is to enable pupils to become independent learners; the same should be true for teachers. Middle leaders should therefore see themselves as 'activators', encouraging their colleagues to strive for constant improvement in a non-threatening environment where weaknesses are acknowledged without fear of recrimination and improvements are jointly planned. Some colleagues will need more support than others, and some may need senior management involvement if the quality of their teaching is well below expectations, but improvement is only possible if there is a strong culture of collaboration and support. And, of course, middle leaders should encourage colleagues to observe their lessons on a regular basis.

Time will always be an issue. Few schools nowadays can afford to release teachers from lessons so they can observe their colleagues teach but there are creative ways around this problem. Teachers who are genuinely interested in improving their teaching are usually prepared to give up their free periods to observe other lessons, and it is often possible to ask senior staff to cover lessons so that observations can take place. In many schools, senior leaders are choosing not to send their staff on expensive commercial courses but to the invest the money set aside for professional development in-house, giving teachers the chance to observe each other more often. In the most forward-thinking schools, colleagues are encouraged to visit other schools to seek out outstanding practice. Of course, middle leaders should have been allocated dedicated non-contact time and this should be used as often as possible to observe lessons.

It is not essential to observe a whole lesson, but it is often good to do so. The fifteen or twenty minutes allocated to Ofsted observations offer only a snapshot of the lesson and form part of a much wider view of the quality of education. Middle leaders should take as much time as they need to develop a real understanding of what is happening in the lesson. This makes the subsequent discussions much more successful as the teacher won't need to spend time describing what happened before the observer arrived or after he or she left.

A sure sign of a healthy departmental culture is the lack of interest shown by pupils in observers in the classroom. In schools where collaboration is part of the culture, pupils are used to having additional adults in the room and, indeed, they are comforted by the fact that their learning is subject to quality control. Pupils, of course, provide their own perspectives on the quality of teaching and it is important, therefore, to include discussions with them during observations. These don't have to be intensive – often a quick word will do – but they are extremely useful in engaging the level of interest in the room. They also reveal whether the lessons are always like this or whether this lesson been specially prepared for the benefit of the observer. A thorough observation will also involve looking at pupils' books and this is covered below.

It is important to make notes when observing lessons – most people are unlikely to remember everything they want to discuss later – but these should be brief and to the point. It is not necessary to record everything that happens in the lesson, only key observations. A balance should be achieved between noting the positive aspects of the lesson and areas for improvement. This then gives shape to the subsequent feedback discussion with praise followed by plans for further development.

Schools use a wide variety of templates for lesson observation note-taking. These range from the most basic – lesson, time, teacher, class, positives and negatives – to wildly complicated arrangements which take most of the lesson to fill out. Indeed, some of them take so much time it is not actually possible to observe the lesson. If the school has its own proforma then this is the one that middle leaders will be encouraged to use; if not, then the best approach is to keep things simple. Some schools have a formal document to be completed for performance management purposes but leave everyday observations to individual departments to sort out. As ever, the best solution involves compromise, with senior leaders insisting on the consistent use of performance management forms, but allowing everyday monitoring forms to be adapted to suit the needs of the subject or the department.

The nature of the notes taken is also important. They should be evaluative rather than descriptive. There is no point writing down what happened in the lesson – the teacher and the observer both know what happened – but it is important to evaluate the quality of what was seen. Experienced middle leaders should also be able to make suggestions for improving the learning: slight tweaks to strengthen the pace, alternative approaches, useful support materials etc.

It is sometimes useful to have a particular focus for the lesson observation. In some schools, this may take the form of a key development plan issue on which middle leaders have been asked to focus; in others, it might be left to departments to decide where to lay most emphasis. For example, a school where the gap between disadvantaged pupils and their peers is large, middle leaders might be asked to pay particular attention to the progress of pupil premium students during their observations. A department-led focus might involve something much more subject-specific – pupils' understanding of the vocabulary used in examination questions in maths, for example.

Lesson notes should not be secret documents; they should be shared with the teacher observed and a copy given to him or her after the lesson. It is good practice to include a section on the back of the form where the subsequent feedback discussion can be summarised and agreed development points recorded.

The discussion following a lesson observation is as important as the observation itself, and should not take the form of a hurried exchange at the end of the lesson as the teacher is preparing for the next class. Time should be set aside so that the lesson can be analysed in detail. This gives the teacher the opportunity to correct any misapprehensions on the part of the observer, and to explain how this lesson fits in with the planned sequence of lessons. In departments where lesson monitoring is accepted as standard practice and far from punitive, these discussions can be fascinating. They often move from a simple analysis of what went on in the lesson to complex explorations of educational pedagogy.

The information gained from lesson monitoring can be used to inform planning for professional development. One of the key duties of middle leaders is to oversee the development of colleagues in their departments. This should involve not only simply asking them what courses they fancy going on, but also addressing particular needs. Regular lesson observation allows these needs to be identified so that training can be provided to enable colleagues both to address areas of weakness and expand areas of strength.

Lesson monitoring is therefore fundamental to improving the quality of teaching and should be seen as a key part of every middle leader's role. It is also, it should be noted, potentially one of the most enjoyable parts to the job. The chance to observe good teaching in practice and to share in a colleague's enthusiasm for their subject is a real privilege.

26

What do I do if my department is underperforming?

There will be times, no matter how strong the leadership, when a department will underperform. There will be years when outcomes are not in line with predictions and years where unavoidable difficulties have impacted on pupil performance. Real problems arise, however, when outcomes are well below national standards for an extended period or when one subject falls below the standards set by other subjects in the school. It is important not to leap to conclusions, however. A department achieving good outcomes against national standards but falling below the standards attained by other departments in the school is not necessarily underperforming. For example, examination boards have traditionally made higher grades in modern languages exceptionally difficult to attain and even the best teachers have struggled to achieve a similar grade profile to their colleagues in other subjects. Detailed analysis is essential, therefore, before departments or subjects are considered to be underperforming and it is often up to middle leaders to make the case when being held to account by senior leaders.

Middle leaders, of course, know when their departments are underperforming – it is usually fairly obvious in the data and from their knowledge of colleagues – and they will be keen to do something about it. Careful diagnosis of the problem is the obvious first step and there is a distinction to be drawn between underperforming pupils and underperforming teachers. Surely, one might say, if pupils are underperforming then it is the fault of the teachers. That may be the politician's line, but it is not necessarily the case. If, for example, a teacher takes over a class with a high proportion of disadvantaged pupils who have already fallen well behind expected standards, or a class bedevilled by persistent absence, then no matter how hard the teacher works, and how much progress is made in closing the gaps, a degree of underperformance is almost inevitable. Teachers may have high expectations, and have provided a huge amount of support to individuals, but it can be an uphill struggle. They should not, therefore, be labelled as underperforming. Good middle leaders need to be alert to such variations and have a thorough understanding not only of each cohort of pupils, but also of each class. They must not only be familiar with the data but take into account their own and their colleagues' knowledge of individual pupils. This can be difficult in large schools, but there is no getting away from the fact that the most effective leaders really know their pupils.

However, if classes in a subject are fairly similar to one another, and yet outcomes in one are low, then there could well be a problem with the quality of the teaching in that class. Successful diagnosis of the problem will involve both careful analysis of examination and internal assessment data and careful monitoring of the quality of education in the classroom.

What a good lesson looks like, and the importance of lesson monitoring, have been discussed above, and we have seen the importance of middle leaders' knowledge of the strengths and weaknesses of the teachers in their teams. This knowledge is an important consideration when analysing examination and assessment data. How to deal with data is considered in the next section of this book, but it is important to point out here that any signs in the data that a teacher has underperformed must be considered alongside knowledge of his or her performance in the classroom. If most pupils in a class have underperformed across the board, in all aspects of a test or an examination, then there is clearly a real problem which must be addressed as a matter of urgency. If, however, pupils underperformed in only one or two areas, the problem can be addressed by targeted support for the teacher concerned.

Of course, underperformance may not be restricted to one teacher. There could be issues affecting all members of the department. If this is the case, systematic analysis of what went wrong and why will be required. Is the curriculum faulty? Have teachers failed to understand the intricacies of the examination criteria? Are expectations too low? A detailed department review – perhaps supported by senior leaders and/or external advisers – may be necessary.

If underperformance is restricted to one particular teacher, diagnosis of the problem is usually much more straightforward, though not necessarily easy to deal with. New teachers will need particular support in learning how to ensure that pupils are well prepared for tests and assessments, but all teachers have weak spots and areas where their expertise could be improved. An effective middle leader looks closely at the data, compares it with what he or she knows about the teacher concerned, and then draws up plans to help bring about the necessary improvements.

There will be occasions, however, when a teacher's performance is poor, and cannot be ignored. As we saw above with regard to lesson monitoring, some middle leaders find dealing with their colleagues a real challenge, but it must be done. Complacency leads to poor outcomes. If a teacher is underperforming, then steps must be taken to put things right. If the middle leader has identified issues which cannot be corrected by a straightforward programme of CPD and support, then senior leaders must be informed, and competency procedures initiated. This does not, of course, mean dismissal; although it may come to that. Schools and unions work hard to support teachers to get them back on track, and everyone should do their best to see competency procedures as supportive, although this is far from easy. The key point here, however, is that middle leaders must be prepared to make difficult decisions in order to maintain high standards in their departments. The old cliché, 'pupils only get one chance at schooling', is perfectly true: a child's education can be ruined by poor teaching. Middle leaders should therefore never shy away from dealing with underperformance. Indeed, they should be proud to do so.

27
Why is consistency so important?

Developing a consistent approach to learning is a key responsibility of leaders at all levels. Essentially it means ensuring that everyone in the school is moving in the same direction. One awkward oarsman in a rowing team can disrupt the flow of the oars through the water and slow the boat; one teacher out of step with his or her colleagues can slow the pace of school improvement and, in some cases, damage overall outcomes. This may seem obvious, but it is actually quite difficult to achieve in practice. There are always one or two teachers who prefer to do things how they have always done them, and there are those who think they know better than their colleagues and refuse to comply with approaches that have been agreed in meetings. The most difficult staff to deal with are those who seem to agree but, behind closed doors, revert to old habits. Feigned compliance is possibly one of the most challenging problems middle leaders have to tackle.

Consistency is key both to outcomes and progression. If a middle leader has developed an approach to, say, the teaching of fractions which has been proved to be successful, a teacher who chooses a different approach may have less impact in the classroom than other members of the team. This will translate into poorer outcomes for his or her class and, in turn, damage overall outcomes for the school. The lone wolf approach also makes life difficult for colleagues. When a class is handed on to a new teacher at the start of the year, if everyone in the department or subject team has been working in the same way, the transfer will go smoothly, and pupils will continue to progress. If the new teacher, however, has to check what has been learnt, fill in gaps, revise the skills and knowledge which should have been taught the year before, the learning will inevitably be disrupted, and pupil progress slowed. This is an issue both within departments and between departments. A few disrupters spread across the school can have a serious impact on whole school outcomes.

It could be argued that performance management is there to make sure that this kind of thing doesn't happen, but it is easy for staff to 'play the game' and put the performance into performance management. Regular lesson monitoring is therefore essential if leaders are to have confidence in their teams.

Of course, consistency cannot be achieved overnight. It takes a while for even the most competent and inspirational leaders to get everyone onboard. Regular and collaborative team meetings are a good place to start, followed by regular non-threatening visits to lessons. Teachers need to be encouraged to observe each other's lessons, sharing ideas and resources. Hopefully, in this way, colleagues will be more open to changing practice if they can see how it works in other classrooms. People often stick to old familiar ways because they are uncertain how to change them; if they see new approaches in practice, in non-threatening contexts, they are much more likely to reflect on their own practice and try new things.

There will, of course, be occasions when middle leaders will need to step in and insist that members of their teams comply with department and whole school policies. It can be difficult to switch from persuasion to instruction, but it is sometimes necessary. Middle leaders often feel uncomfortable telling their 'friends' in the department that they need to follow instructions, but they have to do it. Leadership can sometimes be difficult and demanding. Leaders who shy away from difficult decisions are not good leaders. If they are reluctant to insist that teachers fall in line, they may avoid an unpleasant confrontation in the short term, but they are storing up problems for the future. More to the point, they could be actively damaging the prospects of young people. Middle leaders are in the fortunate position of being able to ask senior leaders to intervene if disagreements escalate, but the aim should always be first to inspire and engage rather than to instruct. Instruction is a last resort. Good middle leaders rarely have to instruct. In departments where collaboration is genuine members of the team tend to get washed along with the enthusiasm and commitment of their colleagues.

There is, of course, a caveat; the desire to control must be avoided at all costs. Some middle leaders, particularly if they are outstanding teachers, attempt to impose themselves on their colleagues, and insist that their methods are the only methods. A firm approach may initially be needed if the department is underperforming significantly, but an authoritarian approach cannot be sustained for long. A balance is essential if colleagues are to work in a team: their contributions must be valued, and their experience recognised. Team leaders are learners too and the best middle leaders realise that they have as much to learn from their colleagues as they have to teach them.

28

Should I insist on detailed lesson plans, and what about objectives?

Ofsted guidance makes it clear that inspectors will not ask to see lesson plans. This does not mean, however, that plans are no longer necessary. Whatever the guidance suggests, inspectors find plans really helpful in providing a quick overview of the lesson. What they don't want to see – and, indeed, none of us do – are wildly complicated plans that take hours to complete. These may be helpful for trainee teachers in the early stages of their careers, but they are unnecessary for more experienced teachers. They also add significantly to teacher workload. So, what should a lesson plan look like?

First, we need to consider learning objectives as these often get in the way of good lesson planning. In simple terms, a lesson objective describes where the teacher wants to get to by the end of the lesson and is thus the essential starting point. Where it is easy to go wrong is to confuse the aim of the lesson with the activities and the tasks to be undertaken. Far too often, teachers create objectives which merely set out what they expect their pupils to be doing. For example, 'The objective of this lesson is to complete a comprehension exercise based on the third chapter of *To Kill a Mockingbird*', or 'The objective of this lesson is to undertake a practical experiment' etc.

In order to write a meaningful objective, teachers need to think about what they want their pupils to learn. Instead of using the term 'objective', they might be better served by completing the phrase, 'By the end of this lesson the class will have learnt …'. In this form, the objective becomes real: pupils are able to understand from the outset exactly what the lesson is about, and their learning is enhanced as a result. If the objective simply outlines the tasks to be undertaken, they will know what they will be doing but not what they are supposed to be learning. It is important, therefore, for teachers to think carefully about what they want to achieve, and phrase their learning objectives with appropriate care.

In many schools, the policy is to write the learning objectives on the board at the start of the lesson and then to get pupils to copy them into their books. For the objectives to be understood, they don't necessarily have to be written down, as long as the teacher has explained them clearly to the class, though it could be argued that it is useful to have them on display so that they can be referred to throughout the lesson. There is very little point, however, in getting the class to copy them down. Copying involves very little thought and, if done on a regular basis, the exercise becomes meaningless. It is much better to make sure that pupils understand what they will be learning and why they are learning it by means of a brief introduction, followed perhaps by an equally brief question and answer session, rather than the laborious process of writing down an objective that might not be understood. If the school policy is to display learning objectives, then it is the role of the middle leader to visit lessons and to check that they make sense. Are they about learning, or are they lists of tasks and activities?

A good lesson plan has a sharp focus and indicates clearly what pupils will have learnt by the end of the lesson. It sets out the learning in a series of sensible steps and outlines very briefly the activities to be undertaken to achieve the aims of the lesson. It is flexible enough to allow for changes in direction depending on how quickly pupils cope with the learning, and it should also indicate any support that might be required for pupils with special needs, or to ensure that disadvantaged pupils are equipped with the cultural capital they need to keep up with their more privileged peers. There should also be some indication of how the lesson will be adapted for pupils who are likely to struggle, and how those who grasp ideas quickly will be stimulated. As we saw in the section above on differentiation, care should be taken to ensure that activities are differentiated in order to enable all pupils to make strong progress without putting limits on the learning of any pupil in the class. The aim for all pupils should be mastery of the learning, even if some will need particular support to get there.

Most schools have their own lesson plan templates, but it is hoped that middle leaders have some input into their construction. If free to design their own, they should, as always, be kept simple. A comprehensive lesson planning form would probably cover the following:

- What will pupils have learnt/achieved by the end of the lesson?

- Links to previous learning.

- Differentiation/support/scaffolding.

- Literacy.

- How will the learning be checked during the lesson?

And also an outline of the shape of the lesson:

- Starter/recap on previous learning.

- Main episodes.

- Plenary – what has been learnt?

- Links to the next lesson.

Of course, planning templates need to be adaptable. If they are too prescriptive, there is a danger that every lesson will end up following the same format, an approach which inevitably leads to boredom and disaffection.

Beginning teachers will want to think carefully about each section of the plan, and probably write a great deal as a result; experienced teachers will need simply to sketch out their ideas. The aim of a good lesson planning template is to sharpen teachers' thinking so that they really consider how best to deliver the lesson; they do not, therefore, have to spend hours writing it all down. Middle leaders must think carefully about their colleagues' workload and well-being when designing lesson planning forms, but they should not shy away from insisting that lessons are planned thoughtfully and thoroughly. Careful planning is, of course, the key to good teaching.

29

How important are seating plans?

Seating plans are useful, if not essential. They undoubtedly help inspectors and observers find their way around the class, and they serve as useful reminders to the teacher of the needs of individual pupils. However, for the vast majority of the time, they will languish in the teacher's folder on his or her desk.

Plans are important at the start of the year. They help teachers learn names and get to know who's who in the class. Some teachers allow pupils to choose where they sit, others decide themselves based on what they know about the class. As they get to know their pupils better, changes can be made. The real advantage of seating plans, of course, is that they encourage teachers to sit and think about the best place for each pupil, both to minimise disruption and to maximise learning.

They are also really useful for recording key information. Most plans now include indications of pupil groups: SEND, pupil premium, looked after children etc. The teacher should, of course, be aware of individual needs but an aide memoire is helpful, especially when one considers how many classes he or she is likely to encounter during the day, particularly in secondary schools where subjects like music, drama and religious studies are allocated only one lesson a week or fortnight.

Increasingly sophisticated commercial packages are now available, which help teachers produce seating plans which are both detailed and up to date. The best ones connect to the school's information management system, and they can be personalised to ensure that they display only the information teachers find useful. For example, plans can indicate which pupils are in school today, whether they have individual needs, their prior attainment bands, progress scores, predicted grades, etc. Some of them also draw on behaviour records to suggest the most effective seating plans to minimise disruption. For busy teachers, they can save hours of time.

For schools expecting an imminent Ofsted visit, seating plans are undoubtedly a good idea. Although inspectors do not ask to see them, they do find them useful. An inspector armed with a seating plan can quickly find pupil premium pupils, looked after children (LACs), those with special needs etc. and they can move around the class much more easily. As we saw with lesson plans, although not essential, seating plans make life easier for inspectors and observers. Making life easier for inspectors may not be top of a teacher's to-do list but making a good impression on an observer is always important. When an inspector enters a room and is handed a lesson plan and a seating plan, an air of professionalism is undoubtedly conveyed creating a positive impression from the start. And, as we know, first impressions count.

30
How important is questioning?

Effective questioning is one of the most widely studied aspects of pedagogy and many consider it fundamental to successful teaching. It should therefore be central to departmental discussions regarding the quality of teaching, and middle leaders should consider the nature and quality of questioning very carefully when observing colleagues. There is a huge amount of research on the subject but there are a number of points on which there is general agreement. Effective questioning:

- Engages pupils in the learning process.
- Gives pupils the chance to ask questions to clarify understanding.
- Challenges thinking.
- Allows teachers to assess pupil progress
- Develops critical thinking skills.
- Fosters problem solving skills.

Questioning ensures that there is a dialogue between the teacher and pupil. Recent research suggests that dialogic teaching can have a significant effect on pupil progress. A study carried out by the Cambridge Primary Review Trust and the University of York found consistent, positive effects in English, science and maths for all children in Year 5, equivalent to about two months' additional progress.[1] The result was similar when looking only at children eligible for free school meals. As most teachers know, good questioning can really bring a lesson to life. Pupils enjoy asking questions and they engage with enthusiasm in lessons where talk is encouraged.

Asking questions is not a straightforward process, however, and effective questioning involves a great deal of skill on the part of the teacher. Teachers need to learn not only how to encourage questioning but how to avoid dominating the dialogue. Teachers tend to talk too much, thus limiting pupil engagement, and this is a particular problem when they are being observed. I have observed so many lessons where the teacher, conscious of an observer in the classroom, shuts down dialogue, or ends a questioning session too early, because they feel they should be performing their teaching role. Just as pupils begin really to get to grips with a topic, the teacher jumps in with a 'helpful' reminder, thus disrupting the flow of thought almost completely. Often, the intervention is followed by an instruction to 'carry on', by which time any chance of real learning has been lost. Similarly, teachers often ask too many questions without giving pupils the chance to think about any one of them. This kind of superficial, rapid questioning tends to create anxiety rather than a good climate for learning.

The type of question is important. Teachers often rely heavily on closed questions, which result in limited 'yes' or 'no' answers. Closed questions have their uses – particularly with regard to knowledge retrieval – but open questions are much more likely to encourage classroom dialogue. They enable pupils to offer extended answers, to try out their thinking and to deepen their responses. If other pupils then become involved, the learning is likely to move to a much deeper level.

A key skill which teachers should be encouraged to develop is the ability to ask the next question. In order to check that an idea has been understood, a teacher may well ask a question which demands a fairly straightforward answer. The pupil answers easily, and the questioning continues. However, if he or she is asked another question, one which challenges them to think about their answer in more detail, the learning deepens. Others in the class immediately recognise the depth of thought required to respond to the teacher, and begin to increase their concentration levels. A good follow-up question thus has the effect of deepening the learning for everyone in the room.

It is also quite common for teachers to ask the class in general, particularly if they are being observed. This has the advantage of ensuring that the question will be answered correctly, usually by one of the more studious members of the class. Thus, the teacher looks good in the front of the observer and the observer will presumably be satisfied that the class understands the topic and that the learning is moving at an appropriate pace. Unfortunately, neither statement is true. The teacher merely looks anxious, and the observer is not convinced that everyone in the class understands what is going on. It is vital, therefore, that teachers use questioning to involve everyone in the class. General questions should be avoided; specific pupils should be targeted. A teacher who regularly works his or her way round the classroom – but never in a set pattern – has the opportunity both to engage every pupil and to check how much each pupil has understood. Some schools have adopted a 'no hands up' policy to encourage this approach, but no matter how it is done, it is important to ensure that everyone is engaged. A class where pupils know that they can sit back and avoid answering questions is one where progress is likely to be limited. One where all pupils are alert to the fact that, sooner or later, they will be asked to contribute is one where pupils really begin to concentrate.

Of course, teachers who adopt these techniques have to be prepared to adjust their questioning to suit the needs of individuals. Challenging questions can take many forms depending on who is being asked. A teacher questioning low-ability pupils may begin with closed questions to give them confidence and secure their trust, before moving on to more open questions which help to challenge their thinking. It is important to ensure that pupils are never embarrassed by not being able to answer as this is likely to deter them from ever attempting to proffer answers without being asked specifically. Nothing is worse than looking foolish in front of your peers. Bright pupils can be pushed to deepen their thinking, but this too has to be done with care – the aim is to challenge them, not show them up. Skilled teachers therefore are careful to create a climate where everyone's contribution is valued, and wrong answers are never mocked.

It is also important to give pupils time to answer. Anxious teachers often move on to another pupil far too quickly if an answer is not immediately forthcoming. Time is needed for thought and reflection, and many pupils need a moment to frame their sentences before responding. Allowing time for reflection has the added effect of lowering the temperature in the classroom. Pupils become less stressed when they know they have time to think, and are therefore much more likely to engage more positively in question and answer sessions.

Middle leaders need to ensure that colleagues in their departments or subject teams develop their questioning skills. Regular training sessions on questioning are therefore essential. Start with the basics – especially for the benefit of new teachers – and then begin to explore what skilled questioning is really all about. Bloom's taxonomy provides an obvious starting point no matter how well known or even hackneyed this model has become.[2] The distinction between lower-order questions which gauge understanding and higher-order questions which demand synthesis, analysis and evaluation skills reliably leads to thoughtful discussions of effective questioning, particularly if colleagues are asked to provide examples from their own recent practice. Useful too is the consideration of the types of questions that might be asked according to each order of questioning:

- Knowledge: *'Can you remember...?'*

- Comprehension: *'Tell me how this works.'*

- Application: *'Where else have you seen this pattern?'*

- Analysis: *'Explain to me what is happening here.'*

- Synthesis: *'What conclusions can you draw from this?'*

- Evaluation: *'Can you measure how effective this is?'*

In practice, middle leaders need to look for and foster skilled questioning. The following checklist may be useful. Do teachers:

- Regularly use questioning to foster dialogue in the classroom?

- Use questioning to assess pupil progress and depth of learning?

- Allow pupils sufficient time to respond?

- Respond positively and in a business-like fashion to correct answers, and do they take time to ensure that incorrect answers are corrected?

- Ensure that all pupils are involved in questioning, including shy or low-ability girls and boys?

- Vary the types of questions used, including closed recall questions and higher-order questions?

- Allow questioning to deepen learning?

- Avoid cutting questioning short unnecessarily?

- Create a learning environment where all pupils feel comfortable asking questions?

- Regularly ask the 'next question' to truly deepen learning?

Teachers often feel that question and answer sessions should be fairly brief because they need to get on and deliver the syllabus. They often feel that lessons in which pupils do most of the talking don't allow them to demonstrate their teaching skills. From an observer's point of view, however, the best lessons are often those where the teacher asks thoughtful, targeted questions which allow pupils to become fully engaged in the topic, and then allows pupils to keep talking to deepen their learning. The best lessons can be those in which teachers do the least talking. A middle leader who is able to encourage his or her colleagues not to talk so much is likely to run a very successful department.

Notes

1 Education Endowment Foundation. (2020). *Dialogic Teaching.* https://educationendowmentfoundation.org.uk/projects-and-evaluation/projects/dialogic-teaching/
2 Bloom, B.S. (ed.) (1956). *Taxonomy of Educational Objectives: The Classification of Educational Goals, Handbook I: Cognitive Domain.* New York: David McKay Company, Inc.

31
What should I look for in pupils' books?

Senior and middle leaders have always looked at books during lesson observations, but the changes in Ofsted's guidance have made 'book looks' or 'work scrutiny' much more important. Now that inspectors are instructed not to spend time analysing internal data, the work in pupils' books is of paramount importance when determining pupil progress. Consequently, there has been a degree of panic in the profession as teachers seek to understand exactly what inspectors are looking for in their pupils' books. Looked at logically, however, pupils' work is the best place to start when considering not only progress, but also attitudes to learning, the quality of assessment, and the impact of the curriculum on what goes on in the classroom. Middle leaders therefore need to spend more time monitoring pupils' work as well as ensuring everyone in the department has a good understanding of their expectations in this regard.

In most schools, middle leaders use a combination of 'book looks', a brief glance at books during a lesson observation, and 'book scrutiny sessions', more formal occasions when the books of a whole class or year group are collected in and considered in detail. Both should be common practice. Looking at books at in class enables the observer to see the work in context and to talk to individuals about their work. It also ensures that books that are less than perfect have not been 'accidentally' left out of the sample brought along to one of the book scrutiny sessions. The formal occasions enable middle leaders to moderate the quality of work across the subject or department and, if all colleagues are involved, to discuss the issues arising.

So, what exactly should curriculum leaders be looking for when looking at pupils' books?

The starting point is to consider what the book looks like. Has the book been well looked after, and is the work well presented? This may seem to be a trivial matter, but the way in which pupils treat their books says a lot about their attitude to learning. Is there evidence that pupils are putting appropriate effort into their work? If a book is well-kept and neatly presented, it suggests that pupils value their learning; it also suggests that the class teacher takes pains to encourage good presentation.

High expectations are vital to good teaching. It is therefore important for middle leaders to consider whether the work suggests that teachers' expectations are high enough. Are these expectations reflected in their feedback to pupils and is there real attention to detail? There is huge difference between a teacher who checks that mistakes corrected previously have not been repeated, or ensures that common spelling errors are not eradicated, and one who simply marks the work in front of them without thinking about learning over time.

One of the most difficult things for external observers to gauge is whether the teacher is focusing on the correct skills and subject content for a pupil's age or the stage in his or her learning. This is particularly true for senior leaders and inspectors observing lessons outside their own subject specialisms. A subject leader or head of department should have no such difficulty and should therefore be able to make clear judgements on whether the work in books is appropriate for the children in the class. This is obviously key to strong progress. Less confident teachers may be focusing on content which limits learning because it fails to engage or challenge. Conversely, ambitious teachers may be making unreasonable demands. It is particularly important to consider the work done in Years 6 and 7 in this regard. Some Year 6 teachers tend to focus only on what is required for the KS2 tests and fail to challenge their pupils accordingly, particularly if they allow them to 'wind down' after the tests in May. Year 7 teachers sometimes have little knowledge of the standards expected in primary schools and lower their expectations of what can be achieved at the start of secondary school. As we have seen, this can result in a significant disruption to pupils' progress. It is therefore something middle leaders will want to consider with particular care.

Book looks also tells us a great deal about the effectiveness of the curriculum. Do the books, for example, show well-sequenced work? Looking through a book from the first to the last page allows the observer quickly to get an overview of the curriculum in practice. It is therefore easy to see whether topics are well chosen, allowing the learning to build step by step. If knowledge and skills are introduced appropriately and in a timely manner, pupil progress will be evident. Middle leaders should therefore use their knowledge of the work in books to help them evaluate the effectiveness of their subject curriculums. They can also monitor the effectiveness of their colleagues' lesson planning in relation to the curriculum plan.

If the work is sequenced well, and the learning builds step by step, middle leaders should be able to find evidence of pupils recalling prior learning. Written tasks should not, of course, exist in isolation. In books where pupil learning develops steadily over time, it should be fairly easy to find examples of work which refers back to earlier work or which draws upon skills and knowledge encountered earlier in the term or year.

Feedback is covered in detail below, but it is worth noting at this stage that book scrutiny enables middle leaders to gauge its effectiveness, both in terms of overall policies and individual teachers' application of those policies. In simple terms, are misconceptions corrected quickly and do pupils learn from their mistakes?

Books also reveal a great deal about the progress of individuals and groups of pupils. They indicate, for example, whether lower-attaining pupils are catching up quickly enough and whether they have failed to grasp concepts or secured essential skills. Is there evidence of additional work to help them consolidate their understanding? Similarly, are disadvantaged pupils and those with special educational needs and/or disabilities receiving work that enables them to make strong progress? Are ambitions and expectations high enough?

A key indicator of the quality of education is progress over time. Books should therefore indicate whether, over time, pupils are making good gains in knowledge, understanding and skills and, where appropriate, catching up quickly to the expected levels of attainment for their age.

Middle leaders should also be aware that the quality of work seen in books says a lot about their own leadership skills. If a subject or department is well led there will be a high degree of consistency in the quality of the work seen in books and it will be obvious if teaching is monitored effectively. Inspectors will ask middle leaders about their expectations regarding the work in pupils' books in order to test their self-evaluation skills. Regular book looks and formal book scrutiny sessions should therefore be high on the middle leader's to-do list.

To summarise, middle leaders should be asking the following questions:

- Is work well-presented and completed, and does it indicate good or attitudes to learning?

- Does the work demonstrate the teacher's high expectations of all pupils?

- Is teaching focusing on the correct skills and subject content for pupils' ages/ stages?

- Do the books show well-sequenced work?

- Are pupils able to recall prior learning in later tasks?

- How effective is the use of assessment?

- Is feedback given regularly, does it demand active responses, and is it deepening pupils' understanding?

- Are lower-attaining pupils catching up quickly enough?

- Are disadvantaged pupils, and those with special educational needs, receiving work that enables them to make strong progress?

- Does work show that, over time, pupils are making good gains in knowledge, understanding and skills?

32
What does good feedback look like?

As we saw in the section above on assessment, there is a great deal of confusion surrounding the terms we use to describe the ways in which teachers respond to pupils' work. The distinction between formative and summative assessment has already been discussed but we now need to tackle the blurring of the lines between assessment and feedback and, of course, assessment and marking. Formative assessment is a diagnostic tool which allows the teacher to check what pupils have learnt. Feedback is one response to formative assessment, but it is not the only response. Teachers who, thanks to regular formative assessment activities, have identified areas of weakness, or gaps in understanding, draw upon a wide range of techniques to revisit the learning and make sure it becomes more secure. Topics can be returned to and the learning reinforced; new activities can be devised to approach the learning in different ways; and new resources can be introduced. Feedback, nevertheless, is probably the response to formative assessment which teachers use most often.

The effective use of feedback depends upon a strong learning culture. If pupils genuinely want to learn, they are much more likely to take feedback seriously. Teachers, too, need to understand the importance of building a learning culture so that every activity builds towards further learning and there is a strong sense of people moving forward together. Pupils should be learning with their teacher; it should not be a matter of following instructions. It is also important for the teacher to have high expectations with regard to the ways in which their pupils respond to feedback. Some teachers have very low expectations and assume that pupils will be prepared to do very little, but if the learning culture is strong, there is no reason why pupils cannot be expected to do more, and thus take charge of their learning.

Feedback is not just about the teacher's marking. Comments written by the teacher in response to a piece of work can be very helpful, provided the pupil takes them on board and does something with them, but other forms of feedback can be equally valid. Oral feedback is often more personal and much more likely to spur people on to further learning. Recently, and largely in response to concerns regarding the supposed need to demonstrate that feedback is taking place during inspections, teachers have resorted to recording such interactions ('Verbal Feedback Given' stamps are now quite common). This makes some kind of sense but the real test of whether feedback has been given is evidence of a response from the pupil which indicates that he or she has taken it on board and thus made progress in learning.

From a parent's point of view, feedback usually means marking. Parents expect to see their children's books marked. It reassures them that the teacher is doing his or her job properly, and a lack of marking can lead to endless complaints or mutterings in the community about feckless teachers doing nothing with their time. Parental pressure often drives senior leaders to introduce strict marking policies to ensure that teachers mark books more regularly. This not only leads to a dramatically increased workload, but also ultimately tends to undermine the feedback process itself. Teachers forced to spend hours marking end up covering books in red ink and writing fairly meaningless comments at the end of each piece of work; comments which pupils generally ignore. Parents need to be reassured, therefore, that feedback is taking place, even if it doesn't take the traditional form of the marking they remember from their school days.

Marking is simply that – marks on a page. Teachers who have been in the profession for a long time find it hard to resist, and often feel that they are letting the class down if they don't tick everything regularly. Middle leaders, therefore, need to ensure that their colleagues move beyond this simplistic approach – and this may mean protecting them from concerned parents – in order to make better use of their time and bring about better outcomes for pupils.

Written feedback should encourage pupils to re-engage with their learning. Comments such as 'Good work but check the spelling' are pointless because pupils do nothing as a result. They may make a desultory survey of their work to see what mistakes they have made but they are unlikely to make an effort to put things right. The most effective examples of feedback force pupils to think about their work and actively engage. Instead of correcting them, a teacher who has spotted a number of spelling errors might write something like, 'Look again at the first two paragraphs and underline the three words you have misspelt. If you get stuck, ask your neighbour to help you.' A maths teacher who has set twenty questions for homework might, instead of marking 16 right and 4 wrong, write, 'You have done really well here, but four of the questions are wrong. Can you find them and answer them correctly?' In both examples, pupils are encouraged to look closely at their work, seek out the errors and correct them. In doing so they will be actively engaged and far more likely to remember what they have learnt and much less likely to make the same mistakes again.

Good feedback therefore encourages active responses. These can fairly brief, like the examples given above, or much more involved. Pupils enjoy being challenged and if the teacher feels that an alternative approach to a piece of work will lead to greater understanding, then he or she is perfectly justified in setting an extended task which will take time for the pupil to complete. A maths problem may have been solved correctly, but if the teacher asks pupils to come up with another way of solving the same problem, the learning will be much deeper. This is what the term 'mastery' is all about.

Pupils need time to respond to feedback, but as we saw in the section above on assessment, it must be purposeful time. The 'ten minutes of planned feedback' at the start of every lesson quickly becomes routine and, as a result, pupils engage less thoroughly with their work. Time should be allocated according to the level of the response required and not just at the start of lessons. It is up to the teacher to decide when activities resulting from his or her feedback will be most effective and how much time will be needed to help secure the learning. If the mistakes or misconceptions are simple, ten minutes may be enough; if there are some serious misunderstandings, or gaps in knowledge, the teacher may decide to plan a whole series of lessons to put things right.

Oral feedback is a regular feature of most lessons. It is evident in teacher questioning and in his or her work with individuals. Whole class feedback be useful if everyone in the class is attentive and fully engaged but it is likely to be lost on many of them. Individual feedback is much more powerful. Some teachers now record this with a note in a pupil's book, or some kind of stamp, but its impact is evident in other ways. It can be seen in the progress pupils are making and it becomes quickly evident to anyone observing the lesson that pupils are responding and therefore learning. Engaging with pupils individually is a powerful tool: personal contact creates an instant connection and the level of concentration increases. Pupils respond positively to personal attention because it makes them feel valued. They are much more likely to remember a personal conversation than a general address to the whole class.

Peer assessment can lead to helpful feedback but, for it to be effective, pupils need to be trained to offer sensible comments and useful prompts to further learning. Remember that many of them are used to seeing the somewhat pointless and anodyne marking of some of their teachers and, without proper instruction, they resort to the same banalities. Time must be taken therefore to help them understand what good feedback looks like. This will involve careful teaching but pupils who understand how to give effective feedback are likely to appreciate and respond to their teachers' feedback more readily.

Whether the feedback is written or oral, it is vitally important to make sure that pupils do actually respond. If teachers write comments in books that ask for some kind of a response, they must ensure that a response is made. Similarly, if a mistake has been pointed out and corrected, either by the teacher or, preferably, by the pupil, then it shouldn't recur. If a pupil's book is full of repeated errors, it is a sure sign that their learning has stagnated. A key task of middle leaders, therefore, is to review books regularly to check to see that pupils are responding to and learning from feedback.

Most teachers offer feedback on summative assessments, but care must be taken here. Tests and examinations are not designed to be diagnostic; they are designed to measure learning, and to be marked and graded. The most useful feedback should once again be driven by an active approach. If a student has got a question wrong, or answered poorly, it is necessary to point out their errors but getting them to repeat the question won't really help. Getting them to do a similar question, once they have understood where they went wrong, is likely to lead to a much better learning experience.

Middle leaders need to develop a good understanding of the most effective forms of feedback and these need to be shared with the teachers in their subject areas or departments. Lessons should be monitored regularly, and books scrutinised closely in order to ensure that feedback is given effectively, thus deepening pupils' learning and enabling them to make strong progress.

33

How important is pupil voice?

Most schools now include pupil voice in their school improvement strategies; how many give it the weight it deserves is another matter. If one thinks about it for a moment, who better to comment on the quality of education than those on the receiving end? Taking the comments of pupils seriously is fundamental to any improvement strategy and middle leaders should therefore take time regularly to interview students and listen to their views. This doesn't always have to be a formal activity – the comments picked up in a walk around the class can be very telling – but it does have to be regular as opinions change to reflect the current climate of learning.

It is important to make sure that the voices of all pupils are heard. In too many schools, the views of the school council are taken to represent the views of the entire student body and this can be a mistake. School councils usually comprise carefully chosen pupils who work hard, who are compliant and who enjoy school. Consequently, the views gathered are often closely aligned with those of the staff and tend therefore to be generally very positive. It is much better to seek the views of a mix of pupils, and particularly the views of 'difficult' and disaffected pupils. They are much more likely to say it how it is, and they usually don't hold back. The polite, compliant members of the school council are unlikely to criticise a particular teacher, or express their contempt for a specific teaching technique, whereas those less enthused by the whole notion of education are usually prepared to say exactly what they think. Of course, their criticisms have to be taken with a pinch of salt, but they are usually not too far off the mark.

Senior leaders tend to ask general questions about teaching, behaviour, bullying, safeguarding etc. Middle leaders are able to be much more specific and focus solely on the teaching of their subjects. This means that a great deal of information can be gained if questions are asked carefully enough. Pupil voice is particularly useful when evaluating new courses, new pedagogy, or new resources. It also gives middle leaders a good idea of how the teaching in their department is regarded by pupils. Of course, teachers must not feel that their heads of department are using pupils to spy on them; they must be involved in the process and be encouraged to understand that the aim is not to criticise or undermine their professionalism but to improve pupils' learning experiences. The focus is not on individual teachers but pupil progress. Once again, we return to the importance of a strong learning culture. In departments or subject teams where teachers focus relentlessly on improving their teaching, the views of pupils are highly valued, no matter how critical, and the role of the middle leader in facilitating the expression of those views is recognised and understood.

Some middle leaders convene regular student focus groups – subject teams – to give regular feedback on their learning. Such groups, if they include a variety of pupils, can be very useful indeed but their responses are likely to be very general. It is better to assemble various groups of pupils on an ad hoc basis to explore particular issues, or even one issue. Suitable discussion topics could include:

- Group, pair or individual work.

- Homework.

- Marking and feedback.

- Challenge.

- Support.

- Choice of resources.

- Progress.

- Rewards.

- Behaviour.

- Assessment.

- Enthusiasm.

It is also possible to dig down into the details of the curriculum to find out what pupils find difficult and the things they really enjoy. An English teacher might, for example, discuss a particular text with pupils: does it interest them, is it too easy to read or is it challenging, what are they learning as a result of reading it? Similarly, a geography teacher might perhaps discuss a unit of work based on a particular country and ask similar questions, in particular the relevance of the topic to their own lives. A language teacher might spend time exploring the impact of oral work: do pupils enjoy it, are they embarrassed to speak in class, does everyone participate?

More general conversations also have their uses, and these are the ones pupils are likely to have with Ofsted inspectors during 'deep dives'. Middle leaders would be wise to rehearse such conversations on a regular basis with different groups of pupils in order to get some idea of the likely responses. They will then be able to address any concerns raised, if there are any, and be well prepared for an inspection when it arrives. The aim is to ensure that there are no surprises when the inspector feeds back the views of the pupils he or she has interviewed.

Individual inspectors choose their own questions, and each goes about things in their own way, but a typical subject discussion is likely to seek answers to the following questions:

- What are you studying at the moment?

- What did you study last term?

- What do you most enjoy about the subject?

- What do you find difficult?

- Can you think of one really good thing about the subject?

- Can you think of something that could be better?

- Do you get help from your teachers?

- What is marking and feedback like?

- Are you encouraged to check your mistakes and correct errors?

- How do you know you are making progress?

- Do you know how well you are doing?

- Does your teacher check to make sure you understand?

- What happens if you miss a lesson and have to catch up?

- Does the behaviour in lessons help you to learn?

- Does the teacher pay attention to your spelling and grammar?

In addition, Ofsted inspectors will ask more general questions to explore personal development, behaviour and welfare. It is important for middle leaders to consider these as well. They might include:

- What is behaviour like in the school? Do you feel safe here?

- Is there any bullying?

- Do you feel safe online?

- Do you learn about topics like British Values and radicalisation?

- Do you get help with your next steps and your future?

- Are you looking forward to moving on to your next school/college/university?

- What about extra-curricular activities?

■ What should I know about the school?

■ Is the school improving?

Subject surveys can also be useful, particularly if they are anonymous. Pupils sometimes feel constrained when talking to adults and avoid saying anything critical in case they face some form of retribution. This is, of course, highly unlikely but it doesn't stop pupils worrying. They are more likely, therefore, to express their views more openly if they are confident that their responses will remain anonymous. Good surveys therefore stress anonymity. The key to acquiring useful information is the careful choice of questions and if a middle leader decides to survey a class or a year group, he or she needs to think about exactly what information it is hoped to gain and shape the questions accordingly. Discussion activities are more likely to provide detail but well thought out surveys can give a good overview of the strengths and weaknesses of a department and are therefore well worth doing. Most good departments conduct an annual survey, and this helps to shape the next departmental improvement plan. Of course, written surveys rarely uncover what good discussions sometimes do: an issue that nobody has thought about, or something which nobody in the department regarded as an issue but which is clearly a matter of significant concern for pupils.

Good middle leaders not only know the strengths and weaknesses of their colleagues, but they also understand the pupils in their schools. They talk to them all the time, value their views, and regularly discuss what they have said with colleagues. They use pupil groups not only to evaluate the quality of teaching and learning in their subject areas but to test out ideas and plan for future developments. In other words, they work together with pupils to improve the quality of education.

34

I am not the head of English, so how important is literacy to me?

It is difficult to underestimate the importance of literacy in schools. It is important in every year group and at every level. Whether it is the intensive focus on language acquisition seen in the early years or the attention to detail required in the sixth form, it is fundamental to a good education. There is a particular problem in secondary schools, however, due largely to the move from class teachers to subject specialists. In primary schools, all teachers are teachers of literacy, and pay close attention to spelling, punctuation and grammar across the curriculum; in secondary schools, too many teachers focus exclusively on their specialist areas and regard literacy as the responsibility of the English department. It is also true to say that too many sixth-form teachers shy away from correcting errors in students' written work because they expect them to be fluent and accurate if they are studying A-Levels, something which is often far from true.

Most secondary schools have literacy policies, and many have a dedicated literacy coordinator. Few, however, ensure that teachers in all subjects pay close attention to literacy, and pupil progress suffers as a result. Primary teachers work intensively to help children develop skills in English, but it cannot be assumed that their literacy learning is complete by the time they start secondary school. The evidence of poor levels of literacy is everywhere. The common errors seen in Year 7 books are often to be found in Year 13 examination essays. Traditionalists would go even further and point to declining standards of literacy among teachers. Certainly, as a headteacher, I have often been dismayed by the standards of literacy displayed in letters of application for teaching posts – and this includes candidates for English posts – and, more recently, I have been shocked by the quality of writing in applications for senior positions in schools. One application for a headship I read recently contained thirty basic spelling and punctuation errors – and he still got the job.

It is no good simply lamenting what many see as a decline in literacy levels, however. In many ways, because of the attention given to spelling, punctuation and grammar in primary schools, literacy levels are higher than they have ever been before. Basic literacy has improved dramatically over the past few decades, but further work is needed with regard to the refinement of literacy skills, particularly at secondary level.

Poor literacy undoubtedly holds children back in every subject; not just English. The importance of good levels of literacy is most obvious when it comes to examination questions. All too frequently, pupils who have the skills and knowledge they need to succeed in a particular subject are thwarted by their inability to decode examination questions. In a maths lesson I recently observed, for example, a student appeared to be struggling with the complex maths demanded by a higher-level GCSE question, but when the teacher explained exactly what the question was asking, it was immediately obvious that the student could solve the problem with ease. Her poor literacy had become a real barrier to learning. I then began to wonder how many times during the day, and in how many subjects, was this scenario repeated – and, indeed, with how many students?

It is undoubtedly true to say that most teachers are aware of all this, and yet not enough is being done to address the problem. A strong whole school literacy policy is vital but middle leaders hold the key to improving literacy in secondary schools. The first step is for them is to recognise what has now become something of a cliché: all teachers are teachers of literacy. Virtually all teachers would agree that this statement is true, but all too often they pay it little more than lip service. So, what should middle leaders be doing to ensure that literacy is fundamental to the teaching of their specialist subjects?

First, a bold, regularly updated literacy policy is important. It needs to dovetail with the school's overarching policy but must be refined to be subject-specific. How this is done will vary from department to department, but is should go well beyond a list of key vocabulary. It should be discussed regularly in department and subject meetings to ensure that it is kept firmly in mind and should be refined in response to the careful evaluation of the impact of literacy in the classroom.

Second, the department's feedback policy should include detailed procedures for correcting errors in spelling, punctuation and grammar. Part of the problem in secondary schools is that teachers in, say, geography or science, are often unsure about what they should be doing with regard to correcting literacy errors. This means that subject-specific CPD is required to ensure that teachers feel confident when tackling literacy, particularly if they have doubts about their own spelling ability. Many secondary teachers were undoubtedly thrown by the changes to the vocabulary used in primary schools to describe features of grammar – the notorious 'fronted adverbial' is a case in point – and they should undoubtedly have been involved in the training their primary colleagues received when the new approaches were first introduced. It is important, therefore, to ensure that whole school literacy CPD brings secondary teachers up to speed with the work done in primary schools.

What could be described as the embarrassment factor should be acknowledged when teachers discuss literacy, and middle leaders need to be aware that some of the teachers in their departments may need specific training in literacy to ensure they have the skills to check pupils' work confidently and accurately. Schools are often reluctant to provide basic literacy courses for experienced, well-educated teachers but, in reality, they are needed and, indeed, often quite popular.

As English teachers know only too well, correcting every mistake is not an effective way to improve a child's spelling; the best approach is focus on particular words, especially those that are repeatedly misspelt. Some teachers may not know this, however, or be concerned that they are doing the wrong thing and so avoid correcting any spelling errors at all. Some very basic CPD could therefore be very effective and give colleagues the confidence they need to focus more closely on improving their pupils' literacy skills.

A strong departmental literacy policy must be put into action. This means that its impact in the classroom should be monitored on a regular basis. Middle leaders should not shy away from picking up on their colleagues' lack of attention to literacy or, indeed, their spelling errors, nor should they overlook uncorrected errors in pupils' books.

It is also important to ensure that pupils understand that literacy is considered to be a high priority in every subject. Far too often, pupils make careless errors which they attempt to justify by saying things like, 'This isn't English, this is science, so it doesn't matter.' Consistency across the department and across the school is therefore vital so that pupils know that literacy is important whatever the subject. In schools where staff adopt a consistently rigorous approach to literacy in every subject area, pupils pay much more attention to their writing. They take much greater care and therefore make better progress. They find that they are able to access specialist subject skills and knowledge much more effectively and poor literacy is no longer a barrier to learning.

Of course, literacy is not just about writing. Teachers should not be afraid to correct spoken errors in class discussions and they should aim to ensure that high standards in spoken English are maintained. Children are masters of code switching – they can move easily between formal English and the language of the street or the playground – but there is a danger that in classes where any form of response is accepted pupils will become less and less confident in the use of formal speech. This may appear to create a more positive atmosphere in the classroom, but it will ultimately penalise students when they enter the adult world of work where a degree of formality is essential.

Nor should we overlook the importance of reading. A teacher of PE may see little point in talking to the class about books, but it is important for all teachers to talk about books if a strong reading culture is to develop. Reading not only helps children develop a wider understanding of the world, it helps them acquire the vocabulary they will need to access the learning in every subject they study.

Middle leaders are crucial to the development of literacy, particularly in secondary schools. They should ensure that it features regularly in departmental discussions; they should plan for regular CPD sessions covering not only subject-specific CPD but the basics; they should look for good literacy practice in lessons; and make sure that regular book scrutiny focuses on pupils' use of English. They should also work closely with the head of English and/or the literacy coordinator to help develop a genuinely whole school approach to literacy. Schools with rigorous approaches to literacy enable pupils to make strong progress and to become much more confident citizens.

35

I am a subject leader; should I be responsible for behaviour?

Many years ago, there was a clear divide in secondary schools: heads of department were responsible for their subjects, heads of year or house heads were responsible for behaviour. Something similar existed in primary schools, though it was not as explicit: the class teacher taught, senior leaders intervened. Things are very different now. Behaviour and learning are intricately entwined and cannot be separated out so easily.

A huge amount has been written about behaviour in schools and I don't intend to discuss the most effective methods for controlling behaviour here. Our focus is on the role of middle leaders with regard to behaviour. We have to start, however, with the role of senior leaders. Most of the research into effective behaviour management suggests that senior leaders have the most significant impact. Where schools have well thought out behaviour policies which are put into practice fairly and comprehensively pupils' behaviour is much better than in those schools where senior staff leave it to classroom teachers to deal with any problems. Most teachers complain about declining standards of behaviour – this is true in all schools – and many feel that their senior leaders offer inadequate support. It may be true that behaviour in schools has declined but poor behaviour is far from inevitable. Schools where the headteacher is visible, where senior leaders intervene quickly to support staff, where sanctions are applied quickly and consistently, and where everyone knows what the rules are and, more to the point, that they have to be followed, exist all over the country. Nor are they restricted to leafy suburbs. There are many schools in desperately deprived areas where behaviour standards are maintained at a very high level.

In 2017, the Department for Education conducted a detailed study of behaviour in schools led by Tom Bennet and came up with the following features of effective practice:

- Highly visible school leaders.

- Effectively communicated, realistic and detailed expectations understood by all.

- Highly consistent working practices.

- A clearly understood school culture.

- High levels of staff and parental commitment.

- High levels of leadership support.

- Thoroughness in the execution of school policies.

- High expectations and a belief that all students matter.[1]

An effective behaviour regime is undoubtedly driven by strong senior leadership but middle leaders, both academic and pastoral, are key to ensuring consistent approaches across the school. We have already seen the importance of consistency with regard to pupil progress and the quality of teaching; it is equally important in the maintenance of behaviour standards. Middle leaders are therefore responsible for ensuring that the behaviour policies introduced and modelled by the senior team reach into their classrooms. Since middle leaders visit the classrooms of their colleagues more often than senior leaders, their impact is likely to be much greater. It is therefore part of the role of the middle leader to insist that consistent standards of behaviour apply in every classroom.

Most schools offer guidance to help middle leaders manage behaviour and their interventions are normally part of the whole school behaviour policy. In many schools, for example, there is a simple hierarchy of interventions: the class teacher is responsible for behaviour in his or her class; if a pupil persistently misbehaves, he or she may be sent to the head of department or subject leader; if the poor behaviour continues, it may be necessary to involve pastoral staff or senior leaders. Most heads of department pride themselves on the good behaviour in their departments and work hard to ensure that it remains good. There are, of course, times when the support of senior leaders is essential and there is no point in denying the fact that some pupils behave really badly despite huge efforts to support them.

If a class teacher is clear about behaviour expectations in his or her classroom and knows that the head of department is always available to help them, they are likely to handle behavioural issues with much greater confidence. The important point here is that heads of department are usually close by and a regular presence in the classroom. Most schools now have 'on call' systems which enable class teachers to call for help from members of the senior team whenever they need it, but many see this as a sign of weakness and worry that they will be regarded as ineffective members of staff if they make use of such systems. In departments where middle leaders play a strong role in supporting behaviour, this stigma doesn't exist. Consequently, behavioural issues are likely to be dealt with much more quickly and effectively.

As part of their regular observations and classroom 'drop-ins', middle leaders need to make their expectations regarding behaviour clear to their team. They should not, of course, undermine the class teacher by dealing with behaviour during a lesson observation, but they should include a discussion of techniques for improving behaviour in any feedback. It should be obvious to pupils that expectations regarding appropriate behaviour are shared by all: they should understand their teacher's expectations and appreciate that these will be reinforced by the head of department, the heads of year and the senior team. If standards are to be maintained, all staff must act as a team and it is the duty of middle leaders to ensure that members of his or her department are part of that team.

Behaviour cannot, of course, be separated from the quality of teaching. More often than not, good behaviour is the outcome of good teaching. If pupils are bored, however, and if they are given work that is either too easy or too demanding, they lose interest and seek to entertain themselves in other ways. Well-planned lessons delivered by skilled and enthusiastic teachers help to engage pupils in their learning and minimise opportunities for disruption. If pupils want to learn and are excited by their learning, they are much less likely to misbehave. It isn't all about the quality of teaching, however. All teachers must pay attention to and, if necessary, impose appropriate standards of behaviour. If teachers are too strict and apply the school's policies with a heavy hand, pupils take delight in seeking to challenge and disrupt; if they attempt to win pupils over and treat them like friends, their liberality will soon unravel and they will find pupils taking advantage of their lax standards.

No matter how good the teaching, there will always be pupils who misbehave. We have to be honest and recognise that some pupils are never going to engage with every subject. A potentially disruptive pupil who behaves well in maths because he is good with numbers may find English lessons utterly tedious and misbehave as a result. Even the best teachers fail to engage some pupils. High quality teaching goes most of the way towards high standards of behaviour, but it is not enough on its own. It must be underpinned by the consistent application of the school's behaviour policies. It is therefore the job of the middle leader to ensure that every teacher in the department applies the behaviour policy consistently and, above all, fairly.

Note

1 Bennett, T. *Creating a Culture: How school leaders can optimise behaviour. Independent review of behaviour in schools.* (2017). Department for Education. DFE-00059-2017. p.7.

36

How do I plan effective CPD?

The more one thinks about the professional development of teachers, the more important it becomes. Busy middle leaders struggling with the frenetic activity of a typical school day find it difficult to make time to think about developing the staff in their departments, but time must be found. It is difficult to underestimate the importance of professional learning. The introduction of the five so-called 'Baker days' in 1988 ensured that regular staff development became a fixture in the timetable and yet these days are possibly among the least effective methods of staff development. They are often taken up with whole school administrative tasks. In very few schools are all five days devoted to pedagogy.

Teachers' professional development should be continuous but for many it stops in the first few years of their careers. Teacher training is intensive, to say the least, and a teacher's probationary year can be a real challenge, but, after that, support and training drops away. In recent years, schools have come to recognise the importance of continuing this early training, but it is yet to get much beyond minor packages of support for recently qualified teachers (RQTs). In their book, *The Teacher Gap*, Allen and Sims point out that although teachers learn a huge amount in their first few years in the profession – and they learn it very quickly – the learning curve soon flattens out: 'Most of us would expect to keep getting better at our jobs throughout our careers, or at least the first couple of decades. But the data shows that the typical teacher seems to stop improving far sooner.'[1] They go on to explore very worrying evidence which suggests that a lack of continuing professional development impacts directly on pupil progress. After their first five years in the profession, teachers' expertise begins to plateau.

Professional development must therefore be continuous, and it is left largely up to middle leaders to ensure that it does. The five in-service-training (INSET) days may well cover important whole school development matters but effective CPD is a much more sophisticated undertaking. It needs careful thought and careful targeting. There are essentially three levels: whole school objectives, department or subject plans, and the development of individuals. Middle leaders need to ensure that they help to deliver the whole school development plan, and this is generally done via the introduction of shared team goals. For example, in many schools, teachers are asked to include one of the key school development objectives in their performance management plans. These are then monitored by team leaders who provide appropriate support to ensure their success.

Subject departments will also have their unique objectives. These are often administrative – the successful introduction of a new examination syllabus, for example – but they can also relate either to pedagogy or subject knowledge. A department may wish to develop a particular teaching skill – higher-level questioning, or targeted feedback – or spend time ensuring that everyone in the department is up to speed with a new set of subject skills, perhaps in response to a new syllabus topic.

Leaders at all levels are often keen to focus on improving pedagogy, enthusiastically introducing new ideas and teaching techniques, but many shy away from focusing on subject knowledge. They perhaps feel that they are undermining their colleagues' professional integrity if they question their subject knowledge when, in actual fact, most teachers relish the opportunity to check that they are up to date with the latest learning. The reluctance of leaders to focus on subject-specific knowledge leads, in some cases, to schools where teachers' subject learning stagnates. One of the most obvious examples is in the use of children's literature in the classroom. English teachers tend to stick to tried and trusted favourites. Many rarely read the latest teen fiction, for example. This could be put down to a lack of funding to replenish out of date stock cupboards, but it is more likely to be due to complacency regarding subject knowledge. Middle leaders should therefore make the enthusiastic sharing and updating of subject knowledge a priority for staff development.

Development time will, of course, always be used to cover the various administrative aspects of the work of a subject department: the monitoring of assessments; examination board updates; new resources etc. It is important for teachers to learn about all these things, but they must not be allowed to dominate. The focus, whenever possible, should be on pedagogy and subject knowledge. It doesn't have to be expressed explicitly, however. A departmental discussion about a recent scientific discovery, or an archaeological find, or a new maths programme on the radio, can often develop into an intense and memorable learning experience for all involved. Similarly, a session in which teachers share their most effective lesson plans can lead to detailed pedagogical enquiry.

Objectives for individual personal development are a key feature of performance management but these can be somewhat limited. Most performance management policies insist on just three objectives, one of which is usually a whole school objective. And because these objectives are formal, they tend towards the perfunctory. Teachers, unsurprisingly, seek to negotiate perfectly achievable objectives with their line managers without really thinking about their real development needs. How many teachers actually remember what their objectives are until they remind themselves of them a few days before their annual performance review? Genuine staff development, therefore, generally exists outside of the performance management process.

Professional development depends on a strong learning culture and should be part of the day to day experience of teachers. Although formalised in performance management meetings and INSET days, it is most effective when it is regarded not as something to be done on particular days, or in dedicated time slots, but as an integral feature of professional practice. Teachers should be thinking about what aspects of their teaching they need to improve, or where the gaps in their subject knowledge are, in every lesson. Middle leaders should use lesson observations to help teachers identify development areas and then provide the necessary support. They should also use subject team meetings to consider broader developmental training deriving from what they have seen in colleagues' classrooms.

A great deal of money is spent on commercial training packages, but their value must be questioned. The first thing to ask is, 'Why are we paying for external expertise when that expertise already exists in-house?' Far too often, the skills of existing staff are overlooked in favour of external providers when, in many cases, they will be able to offer training which is much more appropriate to the needs of the school than a generic commercial package. And it will be much cheaper too. There are occasions, however, when an external view is essential. It is always good, for example, to gain an outsider's view of the work of a department, particularly if the consultant in question has accrued a wide range of experience in other schools. It is also important for staff to attend examination briefings to ensure they are up to date with the latest changes and aware of the approaches taken by colleagues in other schools.

Some of the most effective professional development does, however, take place in-house. Coaching is a particularly effective method of personal development and it is one which many middle leaders use to support and encourage members of their departments. In order for it to be effective, however, it must be carefully targeted and focus on deliberate practice. A coaching session is not simply an uplifting chat with a more senior colleague; it is a chance to focus on the development of a specific skill, or an area of weakness, to bring about tangible improvements. Each coaching session must have a specific focus which is then developed in lessons over a period of time – in other words, a teaching skill or technique which is discussed in detail and then practised in class until it is perfected.

Collaborative learning is a powerful way of enhancing a teacher's skills. Working in pairs or threes allows the rapid exchange of information and skills, and the opportunity simply to visit a colleague's classroom can be an education in itself, particularly if that classroom is in another school. Mentoring a younger colleague on an Initial Teacher Training (ITT) programme is also an excellent way of ensuring that a teacher's skills remain up to date. Trainee teachers nowadays experience increasingly sophisticated training programmes in schools or in universities where they learn the latest theory and the most up to date techniques. While supporting their first forays into the classroom, the opportunity to learn from their training programmes should not be overlooked.

It is also important to encourage teachers to get involved in research. The problem with teachers as researchers, however, is the word 'research'. For teachers who enjoy working in the classroom, the idea of spending time gathering data and testing hypotheses is distinctly off-putting. Of course, it doesn't have to be like this. To make research effective in schools, and to build it into the improvement process, a much more straightforward approach should be adopted. After all, the fundamental purpose of research is simply to come up with an idea and then to test it out to see if it works. If teachers are asked to do this, then the word 'research' becomes much less threatening.

One of the most effective ways of building research into day to day practice is the use of trios or, as they are more threateningly known in some schools, triads. There is something about a trio which makes it work. Teachers working in pairs can become too relaxed, postponing meetings, letting things slip, not taking things too seriously. A quartet allows one member of the group to take a back seat: 'Nobody will miss me this week'. A group of three, however, seems to ensure that everyone takes part as no one wants to let the other two down.

It should be obvious by now that effective professional development is indeed a sophisticated undertaking and one which should occupy a great deal of a middle leader's time. Whether it involves working with colleagues to support whole school objectives, identifying specific subject developments, or working with individuals to help them improve their practice, it must be regarded as fundamental to effective middle leadership.

A major meta-study conducted in 2015 for the Teacher Development Trust in England neatly summarises the characteristics of effective CPD programmes and provides a useful summary of this section of the book. CPD is more effective if it involves:

- Longer programmes.

- Follow-up, practice and support.

- Links to everyday work.

- Consideration of starting points, and not a 'one-size-fits-all' approach.

- Peer learning and collaboration.

- Subject knowledge and pedagogy.

- Clear goals.

- Some external input.

- Explicit links between professional learning and pupil learning.

- Classroom practice and experimentation.[2]

The best schools and the best subject departments make sure that continuous professional development is at the heart of the school improvement agenda and the most effective middle leaders make sure that it is part of the day to day practice of their departments.

Notes

1 Allen, R & Sims, S. *The Teacher Gap.* (2018). London. Routledge. Taylor and Francis. Oxon., p. 73.

2 Cordingley, P. Higgins, S. Greany, T. Buckler, N. Coles-Jordan, D, Crisp, B. Coe, R. Saunders, L. *Developing great teaching – lessons from the international reviews into effective professional development.* (2015) Teacher Development Trust.

37

Are visits to other schools an appropriate use of my time?

One of the mistakes worried leadership teams make following a negative inspection report is to close the doors. With work to do to put things right, they argue, staff need to look inwards and concentrate intensively on getting things right at home. This seems like a logical response but once schools begin to cut themselves off from the world standards are more likely to decline than improve. Visits to other schools are essential for staff development and school improvement. The best advice that can be given to leaders of struggling departments is to get out more.

There are lots of advantages to visits to other schools. They offer opportunities to:

- See and not just hear about good practice.

- Talk to colleagues about teaching techniques.

- Compare pupil progress in different settings.

- Gain reassurance and encouragement that one's department is on the right track.

- Take part in moderation activities.

- Share resources and pick up on new ideas.

- Compare curriculum models.

- Plan for future developments.

- Build subject or leadership networks..

- Establish research trios across schools to broaden teachers' experience.

- Share concerns with colleagues external to the school.

- Take a break and recharge one's batteries.

Visits to other schools are particularly important for middle leaders in charge of small departments or, in primary schools, non-core subjects. A head of music, drama or RE in a secondary school may well be the only member of his or her department, so connecting with colleagues in other schools should be considered essential. A primary subject lead responsible for foundation subjects may be confident in history, geography and RE but less confident in music and art. The opportunity to work with a colleague in another school offers the chance to combine expertise, learn from one other and achieve better outcomes for pupils as a result.

Commercial CPD courses are very expensive and they usually take place in cities or large urban centres. Many are only offered in London. This can be a real problem for schools in rural areas. A visit to a local school can be very cost effective, usually involving little more than a day's supply cover. More to the point, colleagues are likely to learn much more from a school visit, especially when the visit can be shaped to meet their particular needs. Teachers who have spent a day in another school often return to their own departments full of enthusiasm and inspired by what they have seen.

As a teacher, a headteacher, an inspector and, more recently, as an educational consultant, I have never visited a school without gaining something from the visit. Although it is always good to seek out the best practice in the local area, it is not always necessary to visit the 'best' schools. Some of my most important learning has been from visiting schools in desperate circumstances. Indeed, some of the best practice I have seen has been in schools in special measures.

38

What do I do when I am not happy with changes to the curriculum?

There will be times when, as a middle leader, one finds oneself at odds with the plans of the leadership team. Curriculum decisions are sometimes made as a result of necessity, perhaps due to poor funding or a lack of staff in the right subject areas, rather than as a response to the needs of pupils. A headteacher may be forced, for example, to cut a language at Key Stage 4, or cut languages completely at Key Stage 2, because a teacher with the necessary skills and knowledge to teach the subject cannot be recruited. Sometimes, however, leadership teams make decisions which are undoubtedly misguided, or which impact on departments in unforeseen ways. There are many middle leaders who have been dismayed by changes to the option system at the end of Year 9, for example, which have resulted in far fewer pupils having the opportunity to take their subjects. In some cases, subjects are dropped at the last minute with very little consultation due to the exigencies of the timetable.

Middle leaders are generally committed to their subjects or areas of responsibility, and, quite rightly, they are keen to fight their own corners. Indeed, this is an important aspect of the role. However, middle leaders do need to think about whole school priorities and to take care not to regard their departments or subject areas as walled citadels under siege by senior leaders. The wider view is sometime essential. There will be times when whole school decisions which impact negatively on individual subjects simply have to be made, and there is nothing that can be done about it. To take the example from modern languages mentioned above, if the Spanish teacher has moved to another school and, despite national and local advertisements, a replacement cannot be found, a headteacher may have no choice but to cut the subject. Such a cut could well devastate a department but, if a solution cannot be found, there may be no choice but to accept it. There will be times when middle leaders simply have to 'get on with it' and make the best of a bad situation.

Such drastic changes are, fortunately, not all that common, even though years of chronic funding have made them much more likely than they used to be. Nevertheless, middle leaders need to be prepared to respond to less dramatic changes on a regular basis. This means that, where possible, they need to make sure they know what is going on in the school at a senior level and they need to be ready to engage with senior leaders as often as they can. Strong headteachers and senior leadership teams consult regularly with their middle leaders – they are, after all, the subject experts – and respond to their concerns. If difficult choices have to be made, they discuss them and explain the thinking behind them. It then becomes the responsibility of the head of department to explain the changes to their colleagues and to work with them to make the best of a bad situation. This is never good in a school but, sadly, sometimes inevitable.

Consultation is always the key. If middle leaders understand the rationale underpinning changes to the curriculum, they are much more likely to make them work. Sometimes, they will be able to use their areas of expertise to suggest changes, or even solutions, which senior leaders will be keen to adopt. The most important thing to remember is that success lies in thoughtful engagement and not angry ranting. A middle leader may be enraged by a proposed curriculum change, charge into the head's office all guns blazing, and be completely ignored as a result. Someone who listens to the arguments, explores the problem and politely suggests amendments or solutions is much more likely to succeed – and more likely to be consulted in the future.

Taking a whole school view is therefore essential to effective middle leadership; it also helps to prepare middle leaders to step up to senior leadership. Working to ameliorate the negative impact of whole school decisions can be very demanding but, to be more positive, difficulties often encourage innovation.

39
Do I need timetabling skills to understand curriculum implementation?

A basic knowledge of how the timetable works is important for all middle leaders. Detailed technical knowledge is unnecessary but a general understanding of how the timetable is constructed is useful when considering how best to implement the curriculum. Very few schools offer middle leaders specific timetable training, so it is always worth spending an hour or so with the person responsible for the timetable to enable a clearer understanding of how it all works. Sometimes, a timetabling decision is made which impacts negatively on a subject area but if a middle leader has sufficient understanding of how the timetable works, he or she can suggest alternative solutions to improve the situation. It is always worth keeping an eye on the development of the timetable as its construction progresses since early intervention is much more likely to result in changes being made. A head of department who turns up when the timetable is about to be published is unlikely to be successful with any proposed alterations.

Before scheduling the timetable, middle leaders should always be asked by the senior leadership team to identify timetabling needs. A timetable for the forthcoming academic year will be written during the summer term once pupil numbers and staffing requirements have been agreed. Leaders will therefore need to draw up a clear summary of subjects, teachers, pupils, time requirements and rooms. Strong links between middle and senior leaders are essential if the timetable is to be constructed to meet the needs of all pupils and all subjects. Middle leaders should keep copies of emails and conversations held with senior leaders because things change and time-tablers don't always remember everything. It can be very disappointing to discover that a key change requested weeks ago has not materialised because it was simply forgotten. Requests or suggestions made in the corridor, or in a brief discussion, should always be followed up with an email.

At some point copies of the 'combing charts' will be issued for scrutiny. Combing charts show how lessons in each subject are allocated across the department. They contain key information:

▇ The subjects to be offered next year and at what level.

■ The time allocated to each subject.

■ How many classes each teacher is to teach.

■ The pattern of lessons across the week.

It is usually then up to the middle leader to allocate teachers to classes. Good middle leaders attempt to be fair to their colleagues, but they also bear in mind their strengths and weaknesses. They also tend to apply a degree of self-control to avoid creating marvellous teaching timetables for themselves at the expense of their colleagues. So, in a secondary school, careful thought needs to be given to who will be teaching GCSE and A-Level classes next year and who will end up with set seven in Year 9. Achieving a balanced timetable for everyone in the department is no mean feat and middle leaders will find themselves using all their interpersonal skills when explaining their choices. Inevitably, some colleagues will feel aggrieved and even slighted but dealing with such issues is a part of the job description. If it is done fairly – if the teacher who misses out on A-Level teaching this year knows he or she will be involved next year – the process can easily be managed. If the head of department keeps all the best classes to him or herself, a lack of confidence in leadership is bound to result.

Teachers can get very possessive about their rooms, so the allocation of rooms needs also to be carefully scrutinised. In many schools, it is not always possible for a teacher to have his or own room, especially if a department has a large number of part-time teachers, and shared rooms will be inevitable. Again, it is important to be fair. Just because a colleague has had the same room for years, it doesn't mean he or she should be able to claim permanent occupation. Some colleagues need to be given priority – newly qualified teachers and those with disabilities, or example – but others should be prepared to move around if necessary. Often, it is discontent over rooming that causes heads of departments more problems than almost anything else, so a wise middle leader spends a great deal of time getting things right.

The combing charts also enable middle leaders to see how well their subject has been timetabled overall and they may wish to ask for amendments as a result. Key questions to ask include:

■ Are all the subjects in the department running or has one disappeared? (When, for example, the numbers of students opting for a particular GCSE or A-Level subject are low, that subject may have been quietly dropped.)

■ How many periods per week or fortnight have been allocated to each subject, and have there been any changes?

■ Does the allocation of lessons allow for appropriate setting?

■ How large are class sizes likely to be?

- Is the pattern of subjects across the week sensible? (For example, in a two-week timetable, are all the lessons for a subject timetabled in one week? Or, is there a long gap between lessons – one on Monday, two on Tuesday and then nothing until the Thursday of the following week?)

- How appropriate are the allocated rooms? (For example, will a class of 30 fit comfortably in a particular room? If access to IT facilities is needed, are they available?)

- Are colleagues teaching the correct number of lessons? (For example, does the NQT have a reduced allocation?)

Middle leaders with a more detailed knowledge will also be able to think about less obvious features of the proposed timetable which may have a significant impact on their subject areas. For example, how have subjects been 'blocked' and does this have an impact on my ability to choose which pupils go into which sets? If an uneven number of classes has been allocated, with, say, two on one side of the timetable and two on the other, what impact will this have in terms of setting?

The key to a successful subject timetable is negotiation. Middle leaders will, of course, want to fight their corners but if they do so without an awareness of how the timetable works and the impact of their demands on other subjects, they are unlikely to get very far. The ability to compromise is essential. Senior leaders will want to ensure that the timetable is the best fit for all subjects; a perfect fit for all of them is likely to be impossible. A skilled middle leader can, however, have a significant influence on the timetable and thus make the implementation of their curriculum plans much more effective.

40

Am I a leader or a manager?

Not so long ago, a head of department would have been described as a manager. The term 'middle leader' is a relatively new addition to the education lexicon drifting down from the language of senior leadership and ultimately deriving from corporate culture. The traditional role of a head of subject was simply to manage a subject, and it took a while for schools to recognise the complexity of a role which clearly involves far more than the simple management of resources and the deployment of staff. In strict terms, there is very little difference between leadership and management. The Oxford dictionary defines a manager as: 'A person responsible for controlling or administering an organisation or group of staff' and a leader as 'The person who leads or commands a group, organisation, or country'.[1] The former controls, the latter commands.

In practice, leadership is all about winning the hearts and minds of colleagues and taking them towards a shared vision; management is largely concerned with administration. Administration is nevertheless incredibly important and likely to take up a huge amount of a middle leader's time so that sometimes leadership feels more like management. In order successfully to implement the curriculum, therefore, good management skills are essential. Even the most charismatic leaders, who may have a powerful vision and the strong support of colleagues, are likely to come unstuck if they can't cope with the basic administrative tasks that keep schools running smoothly from day to day.

Traditionally, effective management depended upon the successful management of staff and resources. It is now a much more sophisticated undertaking with middle leaders expected to perform a frankly bewildering range of administrative functions, including:

- The allocation of staff to classes.

- Oversight of subject timetables.

- Management of resources, including stock, consumables, IT equipment etc.

- Control of the departmental budget.

- Data management including the tracking of pupil progress, identification of pupil groups and attendance information.

- Coordination of support for individual pupils, including supervision of lunch-time and after school sessions.

- Behaviour management and record keeping.

- Oversight of public examinations.

- Health and safety, and risk assessments.

- Responding to the requests of senior leaders.

- Preparation of cover work for absent staff.

- Liaison with governors.

- Dealing with parental concerns and complaints.

- Preparation of agendas and materials for department meetings

- Provision of CPD.

- Management of the department's area on the school website.

- Oversight of departmental trips and visits.

- Attendance at meetings.

- Preparation of the departmental development plan.

- Line management.

- Performance management.

- Evaluation of examination performance.

This is a somewhat daunting list which I am sure doesn't cover everything a head of department is expected to do. It makes it clear, however, that administration is a huge part of a middle leader's job, and thus vital to the successful implementation of the curriculum. The trick, as always, is to achieve a balance between management and leadership. Effective middle leaders are able to combine administrative efficiency and attention to detail with a constant and powerful focus on teaching and learning. Administration is regarded not merely as paperwork but as the scaffold supporting the creation and maintenance of the learning culture.

Department or subject team meetings offer a good example of how to combine administration with teaching and learning. A typical administrative agenda may look something like this:

1) Development plan.

2) Pupil data.

3) Review of resources.

4) Upcoming events.

5) Examination board updates.

6) Any other business (AOB).

Such an agenda may lead to a very effective meeting, but it is much more likely to involve a series of dry and unengaging updates on essential administration. The involvement of colleagues in the department may be minimal a result. The language used also makes it clear that the aim is to get through the agenda as quickly and efficiently as possible so that everyone can go home or get on with their teaching. A more engaging agenda might look something like this:

1) My best lesson this week.

2) Pupil progress, including a book scrutiny (Y9 this week).

3) Curriculum update.

4) Essential admin (data drops, health and safety resources, events, exam board updates, AOB).

5) Discussion topic (e.g. what do we mean by challenge?).

The first item ensures that staff are immediately engaged and encouraged to share good practice; the second focuses directly on pupil progress. Administrative tasks are deliberately placed lower down the agenda so that they can be dispatched quickly and efficiently leaving time for a longer discussion of pedagogy later in the meeting. Avoiding an AOB at the end of agenda allows time for the key discussion to run on as long as colleagues are interested and engaged. In this way, important administrative items are covered but it is crystal clear that this is a meeting about teaching and learning and not paperwork.

Successful middle leaders don't neglect administrative tasks to focus on pedagogy; they understand that administrative tasks provide the foundations for the effective practice of teaching. They are managers, certainly, but ultimately leaders of learning.

Note

1 Lexico powered by Oxford. https://www.lexico.com/definition/leader

41

How do I plan for public examinations?

As we saw in the section above on curriculum, public examinations mark the end-points of education, they are not the sole purpose of education. Nevertheless, it is incumbent upon middle leaders to ensure that both pupils and colleagues are well prepared for examinations and in a position to achieve success. A subject may have a compelling curriculum and a team of first-class teachers but, if scant attention is paid to the management and oversight of public examinations, pupils will underachieve, and the department's reputation will plummet.

The first step is a thorough understanding of the examination in question. This entails reading subject specifications, scrutinising past papers, and becoming familiar with everything the examination board has published. In some cases, there will be no choice with regard to which syllabus to follow – Key Stage 2 tests, for example, or minority GCSE and A-Level subjects – but, for many, the first thing to do is to choose a syllabus. Some departments stick with tried and tested examination boards, but they may be doing their students a disservice by doing so. Subjects where the boards offer a range of syllabuses do so to cater for the needs of different cohorts.

The old distinction between public school boards and those aimed at mainstream education has largely disappeared now but there can be striking differences between the various specifications. The rules are a little tighter at GCSE level, with most boards following common agendas but there can be striking differences at A-Level. It is up to middle leaders, therefore, to think very carefully about which specifications best suit the students in their classes as well as considering the staff expertise required to teach topics effectively.

It is also important to consider variations in results. The Office of Qualifications and Examinations Regulation (Ofqual), which regulates qualifications, examinations and assessments in England, is keen to stress comparability of results across the various boards but, in practice, there is often considerable variation. As most school leaders know, it can be much harder to achieve an A* grade in one board than in another. This is not necessarily because standards vary but because some boards are better suited to some cohorts of pupils than others. If, despite good teaching and thorough examination preparation, results in a department remain low, subject leaders must ask whether they have chosen the most appropriate examination for pupils in their school. Discussion and comparison with heads of department in other schools is really useful here as it allows subject leaders to get beyond the glossy brochures to an understanding of the examination board in practice. Switching examination boards should not be done lightly, however. It is not like switching electricity providers. It should not be done as a reaction to a year of disappointing results but after careful thought and detailed research.

The easiest way to ensure that departments have the up to date knowledge of examinations they need is to ensure that someone in the team works as an examiner. This is not a spectacularly well-paid undertaking – most teachers examine in order to pay for a holiday – but it is a powerful form of CPD. It enables colleagues to be much better prepared and to have a thorough understanding of examiners' expectations. It also ensures that moderation exercises are much more accurate. It should also be noted that middle leaders who ensure that they keep up to date with what the examining boards are doing, don't fall into the trap of teaching texts which have been discontinued or topics which have been withdrawn. Examining boards are generally very good at protecting pupils from the incompetence of teachers but such mistakes should never happen.

In order to ensure that students are well prepared for examinations, middle leaders need to adopt a range of strategies to help develop their understanding of examiners' expectations. This will involve careful analysis of past papers, careful consideration of the exemplars and model answers supplied by the board, review of returned scripts and familiarity with the online review tools which most boards now make available. One of the most significant steps forward in recent years has been the opening up of access to question level detail. Teachers and subject leaders can now delve into the fine detail and identify not only the topics where students underperformed or excelled but the individual questions. Of course, there is no point simply looking and sighing. Once an issue has been identified steps must be taken to put things right. This may involve adjustments to the curriculum, changes in teaching methods, or support for particular pupil groups.

A carefully constructed curriculum, as we have seen, has assessment built into it, and this will, of course, involve assessments which check progress towards examinations. This is done by a combination of regular formative assessment but also by key summative moments. Mock examinations are important in identifying areas of weakness in the run up to public examinations and it essential, therefore, that middle leaders take them seriously. It is not just a question of getting students to sit last year's paper – with so many and such frequent changes to the format and nature of examinations there might not be a last year's paper – but the careful construction of papers which enable teachers to diagnose pupils' ability to cope with all aspects of the syllabus. Papers need to be carefully marked, areas for development identified, then a programme of support put in place across the department.

Finally, middle leaders need to ensure that examination technique is built into the curriculum, and that all colleagues in the department are teaching appropriate and consistent approaches to tackling examinations. Good examination technique can make a huge difference both to individual outcomes and to the overall performance of the department.

42

How important is cross-curricular work?

Literacy is fairly unique in cross-curricular terms in that it has an impact on every subject in the curriculum. Numeracy features in many, if not most, subject areas but it doesn't underpin learning in the way that literacy does. In many ways, literacy sits outside considerations of cross-curricular provision because it is fundamental to every subject. What we are talking about when we talk about cross-curricular working are connections and links between what would normally be regarded as discrete and separate disciplines.

The education system as currently imagined seems positively to discourage a more holistic approach to learning. In secondary schools, the curriculum is divided up into separate subject disciplines and, in most, there is very little contact between the various subject departments. Primary schools, largely because they are organised around classes rather than subjects, have greater scope for cross-curricular connections but as children move up through the school such links gradually lessen and become weaker. Reading, writing and maths dominate primary education and the foundation subjects are given less and less time once the Key Stage 2 tests appear on the horizon. They become the background to the main event.

Pupils are encouraged to regard education as a collection of isolated units. They learn reading, writing, mathematics and 'topics' when they are young; they then progress to English, mathematics, science, history, geography, art, music, technology etc. Often, they simply cannot make connections between subjects and look baffled if they are asked to do so. Anyone who has taught Shakespeare at any level will be familiar with the looks of utter bewilderment on the faces of pupils if they are asked if they have learnt anything in history about Elizabethan or Jacobean England. History is history, English is English. This inability to make connections, however, is hardly their fault since their learning has always been delivered in discrete chunks. Classroom walls are surprisingly thick. When a child enters a classroom, he or she enters a separate world: the teacher is different, the rules are interpreted differently, the pace of learning is different, and the effort demanded is different. All of this serves to reinforce the notion that subjects are different from one another and that they too are separated by the walls of the classroom.

A properly conducted subject audit reveals a huge number of links between subject areas. The search for numeracy across the curriculum, for example, will note its appearance not only in obvious places like science but in measurements in art; calculations in design and technology; in music theory; in grammatical functions; in geography field work; in historical statistics, and so on. Sometimes pupils learn the same things twice but in slightly different ways. I once observed an interesting discussion, for example, between the heads of science and maths who were talking about the way they taught pupils to draw and interpret graphs, a seemingly simple set of skills which, it turned out, they approached in very different ways. As far as their pupils were concerned, there were graphs in maths and graphs in science. That they might be the same may not have occurred to them.

The best schools recognise these issues and seek to make connections between subject areas. They seek out transferrable skills and try to ensure that pupils learn how to connect the knowledge gained in one subject with that already encountered in another. Teachers are encouraged to make links between schemes of work and to help pupils to think beyond the walls of their classrooms. Such an approach undoubtedly has to be led by the senior leadership team but, as is often the case, middle leaders have to make it work in practice. Senior leaders need to advocate cross-curricular thinking; middle leaders need to make the connections.

In the discussion of the curriculum above we considered the importance of sequencing and interleaving. Cross-curricular work demands the same sort of approach but on a much wider scale. It demands the kind of whole school planning which defeats many leadership teams, especially in secondary schools. It can, of course, be done and the result is a much more joined up approach to education which benefits pupils enormously. In schools where cross-curricular thinking is the norm, pupils learn transferrable skills which are reinforced in a range of subjects; they avoid repetition because key skills are taught only once; their learning is given a real sense of context as knowledge sets from several subjects are drawn together; and they appreciate the point of their learning much more readily.

So how do middle leaders go about making connections? In schools where cross-curricular working is in its infancy, the best approach is to start small. A head of science, for example, might begin by sitting down with the head of maths to consider the mathematical skills required in the science curriculum. Once these have been identified, they can be built into both subject curriculum plans and interlinked, thus strengthening the learning in both areas. This might mean a change to the sequence of learning in one or perhaps both subjects, but such changes will surely be worthwhile. Similarly, a head of English might want to work with the head of history to ensure that pupils reading a particular text have the historical background knowledge they need to understand its context. Once such connections have been made, others can be added. What can the art department add to a pupil's understanding of a text studied in English? How can the work done in geography help to enrich pupils' understanding of a scientific concept?

Primary colleagues have considerable experience of drawing together a range of subjects when planning foundation topics. When introducing the Romans, they might cover elements of history (Julius Caesar), geography (Italy), RE (Roman religion), art (mosaics), design (costume making), maths (Roman numerals), science (hypocausts and aqueducts) etc. Whether they then make connections with other topics is another matter. In the same way that secondary pupils tend to see their learning in particular subjects as bounded by the walls of the classroom, primary pupils may regard topics as discrete and separate items if they are not encouraged to make connections between them.

Connections are also important in enabling pupils to remember more. If topics are seen as separate entities, then they can be quickly forgotten. An amusing discussion I had recently with a primary school pupil makes the point. He was currently studying a topic based on Christianity and he was able to explain very clearly, and with a degree of enthusiasm, what he had learnt. However, the term before he had been studying Islam, and he seemed to find it impossible either to recall much of what he had learnt or to compare it with what he was currently learning. When asked what the building equivalent to a church in Islam was, he struggled to think of a mosque. His response to a question about important religious figures resulted in the immediate naming of Jesus and a blank when it came to Islam – a blank, that is, until he suddenly remembered his favourite footballer, Mo Salah. Somebody in his class had obviously linked the sound of Salah with Allah, and this had stuck in the child's mind. Putting aside the bizarre notion of Mo Salah leading a major world religion, it was obvious that the boy was unable to make the cross-curricular connections which would have dramatically enhanced his understanding of RE.

The construction of topics in foundation subjects nevertheless provides secondary colleagues with a good model for the development of cross-curricular links. However, middle leaders in secondary schools need not only to draw together knowledge and skills from a range of subjects, but also to bring their colleagues together in order to make connections possible.

Curriculum sequencing on this scale is obviously a complex undertaking and a perfect model is, in reality, virtually unobtainable. However, if pupils are given enough examples of cross-curricular links, they will begin to regard their learning in a very different light. They will begin to make connections between subjects and thus make much more sense of what they are studying. This approach also fosters independence and is therefore a key ingredient in the creation of a successful learning culture.

43

What about pastoral leadership?

So far, we have been focusing largely on subject leadership rather than pastoral leadership, although many of the questions explored above apply equally to both. This is partly due to the influence of the new Ofsted framework which, with its deep dives and curriculum discussions, focuses relentlessly on subject leaders, but also due simply to the way the education system in the UK is designed. Schools deliver a subject based curriculum; it is therefore academic subjects which constitute the heart of the learning experience. Pastoral leaders support the implementation of the curriculum; subject leaders deliver the curriculum. This is not to devalue the role of pastoral staff, but it does help to differentiate the two types of leadership, especially from Ofsted's point of view. Inspectors do not conduct deep dives into year groups or houses, and they are unlikely to speak to pastoral leaders on the first day of an inspection, if at all. When they do engage with them it is usually to explore issues relating to personal development.

An Ofsted discussion with a head of year is likely to be largely concerned with behaviour and attendance since these are now key inspections judgements. Evidence for the broader aspects of personal development will be picked up from across the school – lesson observations, the work on the walls, discussions with pupils, parental surveys, website information etc. – but if they are explored explicitly with a pastoral leader the focus will be on the EIF grade criteria which seeks to assess the extent to which:

- The curriculum extends beyond the academic, technical or vocational.

- The curriculum and the provider's wider work support learners to develop their character.

- The provider prepares learners for future success in their next steps.

- The provider prepares learners for life in modern Britain.

This approach does not, however, take into account the recent blurring of leadership roles. We have already seen how subject leaders now take responsibility not only for the delivery of the curriculum but behaviour and individual pupil support too.

Once upon a time, it was the job of the head of year to be responsible for behaviour management and pupil support. The role of the pastoral leader was also much more clearly defined. It involved disciplining pupils, liaising with parents, leading assemblies, and co-ordinating PSHE and citizenship. The monitoring of academic progress was left to heads of department and senior leaders. This is far from the case now. Pastoral leaders are responsible for the attainment and progress of all pupils in their year groups or their houses, and they are held accountable accordingly.

Pastoral leadership is now a complex and multi-faceted role, and it is regarded by many as the best way to prepare for senior leadership. A head of year, for example, now needs not only a sophisticated understanding of behaviour management and personal development, but also a detailed grasp of pupil progress data. After a short period in the role, he or she will have gained experience of leading a team, curriculum development, behaviour management, data analysis, liaison with parents, public speaking and high stakes accountability. In other words, the key responsibilities of the senior leadership team.

Pastoral leaders are usually involved in the implementation of key aspects of the PSHE curriculum, but their role is much wider than that and touches upon many of the areas considered above: assessment, progress monitoring, support for disadvantaged pupils, lesson observation and so on. In other words, their work is crucial to successful curriculum implementation, even if it is unlikely that they would describe what they do in that way.

So, what exactly do they do? Essentially, the role of the pastoral leader is one of oversight. Key responsibilities include:

- Supporting consistent standards of behaviour both in the classroom and around the school.

- The construction and coordination of an effective PSHE and citizenship programme

- Liaison with parents.

- The tracking of pupil data across all subjects but with a particular focus on progress towards Key Stage 2 tests in primary schools and GCSEs in secondary schools (which also involves close attention to accountability measures such as Progress 8 and the EBacc).

- The co-ordination of support for individual pupils, including those with special educational needs and/or disabilities, disadvantaged pupils and those who are underperforming.

- Oversight of pupil groups: pupil premium students, those with English as an additional language, LACs, etc.

- Close liaison with other middle leaders including heads of subjects and the SENCO.

- Leadership of tutor teams.

- Monitoring of the work of tutors and the provision of CPD.

- Monitoring of attendance data.

- Lesson visits to observe the behaviour and progress of individual pupils, and to support particular teachers.

In most secondary schools, pastoral leaders stay with a cohort of pupils for several years and perform many of the functions undertaken by class teachers in primary schools. This means that they really get to know both pupils and their parents. This gives them a unique overview of pupil progress and welfare. They support the implementation of the curriculum across a whole year, they have an accurate understanding of overall pupil progress, and they know how pupils behave both in class and around the site. It is surprising, therefore, that Ofsted inspectors don't spend more time with them in order to gain a better understanding of the work of the school.

44

How do I lead in uncertain times?

Schools are places of routine. They have to be. Children need routines. Anyone working in a school becomes so familiar with routines that, after a while, they barely register. School routines are remarkable in their lack of variation. Schools start and end at the same time; lessons take place at the same time every day, and in the same rooms; teachers see the same pupils; they teach the same or similar things year on year; they spend the same amount of time planning and marking; the academic calendar features regular holiday periods at the same times of the year; parents evenings and school events follow a similar pattern every year; and life is punctuated in most settings by the inescapable sound of the school bell. When habitual practices such as these suddenly fall away, life can become very difficult indeed.

The degree of disruption caused to schools by the Covid-19 pandemic is hard to underestimate. For teachers, pupils and their parents, everything changed. The old, stable routines were ripped away and the education system had to be re-thought virtually overnight. It is fair to say that most of the responsibility for managing such sudden change fell on senior leaders, but middle leaders were also forced to adapt to working in ways they had probably never even thought about before.

Headteachers were presented with problems that were often almost impossible to solve. They had to deal with partially open schools, staff working from home, online learning, limited access to disadvantaged pupils, severe social problems, parental concern, political pressures, and fantastic uncertainty with regard to planning for the future. However, with astonishing adaptability, schools were able quickly to set up home learning networks, and staff soon became adept at online teaching. Many schools went to huge lengths to protect vulnerable pupils and many found themselves at the heart of community efforts to ride out the storm. And yet, despite all this, far too many pupils fell behind with their studies, and far too many simply were unable to, or chose not to, engage with online learning. Lessons will undoubtedly be learnt, and it will be important for schools to be prepared for similar periods of disruption in the future. It may even be the case that many of the changes that teachers have long been calling for begin to be put in place as the educational landscape is reshaped for a very different future and a very different society.

Middle leaders therefore need to think carefully about the ways in which their roles changed under lockdown and to ensure that they are ready to respond to similar events in the future should they occur. The question leaders are now most likely to be asked in job interviews will surely be, 'How easily can you cope with change?' Adaptability will be a key requirement of any leadership role and a skill that some will need to cultivate in order to thrive in the educational landscape of the future.

When schools were closed, middle leaders suddenly found themselves presented with an enormous number of problems to solve. Many of these were worked through with senior leaders but many were left to middle leaders to sort out on their own. These included

- How to work from home.

- Keeping safe if still in the classroom.

- Encouraging and supporting colleagues in their departments.

- Quickly adapting to online learning.

- Becoming not only familiar with online learning platforms but sufficiently skilled in order to support members of their subject teams.

- Re-thinking lesson planning to ensure that pupils participated and then remained engaged.

- Co-ordinating teaching across the team to ensure that standards were maintained.

- Adapting the curriculum to enable online delivery.

- Ensuring that the work done by children of key workers in school was kept in alignment with the work done by pupils at home.

- Development of online or telephone CPD sessions to support colleagues.

- Liaison with senior staff at a distance.

- Parents evening conducted by email.

- New approaches to assessment, both formative and summative.

- Developing a greater understanding of mental health issues resulting from social isolation both for pupils and teachers.

Perhaps the most significant change resulted from the cancellation of public examinations. Primary colleagues were fortunate in that the Key Stage 2 tests could easily be replaced by teacher assessments which many believe to be more accurate anyway, but secondary school teachers were faced with the need to assign GCSE and A-Level grades which could have life changing consequences for the pupils involved. Suddenly, the predicted grades which all teachers submit to examining boards, and which are known to be wildly unreliable, had to assess pupils' ability as fairly and as accurately as possible. Middle leaders were responsible for moderating these grades, and many will have found this difficult to say the least, especially via the internet rather than face to face. They will also have been aware that their work would then be subject to senior leadership moderation in order to ensure a consistent approach across the school, followed by examining boards and Ofqual adjustments. New skills would undoubtedly have been learnt during this process, and new challenges faced, many of which may well become part of a new pattern of work in the future.

It is, of course, important to stress the positives here. Middle leaders certainly faced an uphill task in having to adapt so suddenly to new responsibilities and changes to their patterns of work but, in doing so, they may well have equipped themselves to cope more effectively with a new educational and pedagogical landscape. There is also the possibility that schools may change in positive ways, with many of the improvements longed for by teachers at last put in place. Perhaps the most positive outcome of all will be a change in public and political attitudes to the teaching profession resulting in the enhancement of the professional status of teachers. Parents who struggled with home schooling and enforced child minding, and politicians who, for the first time, were forced to think seriously about the complexities of a teacher's job, may well have learnt that teachers are more valuable and much more highly skilled than they ever realised.

The Covid-19 crisis may well have changed education for ever, and it has certainly forced middle leaders to adapt to completely new ways of working, but the essentials remain the same. Leaders' intentions haven't changed, but the implementation of those intentions has undoubtedly become more complicated. The lasting effects of such a long period of disruption won't be fully understood for years but their impact on children's education is already obvious, not only in examination outcomes but in the gaps in their learning. With this in mind, it is now time to move on to consider the role of middle leaders with regard to the impact of the curriculum.

3 IMPACT

45
What is meant by impact?

The most obvious way to assess the impact of the curriculum on pupil progress is to look at performance data. The introduction of national performance measures meant that a very narrow range of data gained prominence in schools as senior leaders were encouraged to focus relentlessly on phonics, Key Stage 2 test scores, GCSE and A-Level outcomes, and, more recently, Progress 8. However, impact is about much more than the measurement of data and can be seen in lots of other ways, many of which are difficult to measure. Teachers who remember the moments when children's faces light up with understanding know all about impact. They also see it as their classes make steady progress across the year, and when pupils show confidence in demonstrating new skills or proudly show off their newly acquired knowledge. This is the kind of impact that brings people into the profession and, indeed, keeps them there, but it can be very difficult to quantify. Consequently, as far as politicians are concerned, the only reliable ways to measure impact are data based.

To be fair to Ofsted, the new inspection framework attempts to shift the focus away from hard data per se towards a broader consideration of what pupils have learned. Published data is, of course, to be considered, but it is only one aspect of the inspection process. The pledge to avoid internal school data is particularly significant because it allows much greater emphasis to be given to the work taking place in the classroom. This is surely a change to be welcomed, even if inspectors are still likely to enter schools with their heads full of the most recent performance data which may, in some circumstances, cloud their judgements.

The EIF outlines clearly the evidence base inspectors will use to judge impact. Inspection experience and research show that the most important factors to consider are that:

- A well-constructed, well-taught curriculum will lead to good results because those results will reflect what pupils have learned. There need be no conflict between teaching a broad, rich curriculum, and achieving success in examinations and tests.

■ Disadvantaged pupils and pupils with SEND acquire the knowledge and cultural capital they need to succeed in life.

■ National assessments and examinations are useful indicators of pupils' outcomes, but they only represent a sample of what pupils have learned. Inspectors will balance outcomes with their first-hand assessment of pupils' work.

■ All learning builds towards an end point. Pupils are being prepared for their next stage of education, training, or employment at each stage of their learning. Inspectors will consider whether pupils are ready for the next stage by the point they leave the school or provision that they attend.

■ Pupils in sixth form are ready for the next stage and are going on to appropriate, high quality destinations. Inspectors will also consider this.

■ If pupils are not able to read to an age-appropriate level and fluency, they will be incapable of accessing the rest of the curriculum, and they will rapidly fall behind their peers.[1]

Senior and middle leaders trained to prepare for Ofsted inspections by careful analysis of performance data, supplemented by the careful presentation of internal data sets, now need to pay much more attention to the curriculum and the effectiveness of its implementation in the classroom. Of course, there is a tension here. Performance tables still exist, and they exert a powerful influence over schools, parents and politicians. Ofsted inspections may well prioritise the curriculum to judge a school's effectiveness, but it is pupils' performance in Key Stage 2 tests, GCSEs and A-Levels which features in the newspapers.

The EIF acknowledges that inspectors will use the official School Inspection Data Summary Report (IDSR) as a starting point but it emphasises a new approach which allows inspectors to 'get to see first-hand the quality of education as experienced by pupils and understand how well leaders know what it is like to be a pupil at the school.'[2] In other words, data is still important but so is the curriculum. Middle leaders therefore need to have a good grasp of the data, but they must also think about the ways in which the impact of their work on implementing the curriculum can be seen in the classroom. The EIF is quite helpful in outlining how inspectors go about gathering evidence specific to curriculum impact, explaining that it will be drawn from the following sources:

■ The progress that pupils are making in terms of knowing more, remembering more and being able to do more.

■ Nationally generated performance information about pupils' progress and attainment. This information is available in the IDSR, which is available to schools and inspectors, and will be analysed for its statistical significance in advance by Ofsted's data and insight team.

- First-hand evidence of how pupils are doing, drawing together evidence from the interviews, lesson visits, work scrutinies and documentary review.

- Nationally published information about the destinations to which its pupils progress when they leave the school.

- In primary schools, listening to a range of pupils read.

- Discussions with pupils about what they have remembered about the content they have studied.

- How well pupils with send are prepared for the next stage of education and their adult lives.[3]

Inspectors look at progress in class, national data sets, pupils' books and destination data. They observe lessons, talk to pupils, paying close attention to particular groups, and they look at documents relating to the curriculum. At the heart of this approach, however, is an intense focus on what pupils have learned: do they know more, can they remember more, and can they do more? In other words, the three things all good teachers check for in every lesson.

Notes

1 *The School Inspection Handbook* (September 2019). 190017. Crown Copyright 2019, p.46.
2 Ibid. p.47
3 Ibid. p.48

46

How do I measure pupil performance?

The measurement of pupil performance involves a combination of hard and soft data. Middle leaders must look in detail at the performance data relating to the pupils in their care, but they must also be able to make judgements regarding progress in other ways. The guidance given to inspectors above points the way.

Data analysis is the first step (see below) but the range of data available will vary from subject to subject. In primary schools, middle leaders are able to analyse early years foundation stage data, phonics and multiplication table outcomes, Key Stage 1 assessments and Key Stage 2 tests, but these cover the core curriculum areas only. Data relating to foundation subjects is harder to come by.

Similarly, in secondary schools, heads of English and maths have access to a huge amount of data, whereas heads of non-core subjects have much more limited data sets to explore. Finding out exactly what data is available is therefore essential. A head of English is able to use the IDSR, national performance tables, and the online analytical tool Analyse School Performance (ASP) which replaced RAISEonline (Reporting and Analysis for Improvement through Self Evaluation) in 2017. Heads of other subjects are limited to subject specific data provided by the school, local authority or trust, as well as commercial systems such as SIMS (School Management Information System) and SISRA (Service for Improved Schools' Results Analysis). The most useful source of data for non-core subjects, however, is probably the analytical data produced by the examining boards.

In addition to the data, middle leaders will need to develop systems to enable them to assess pupil performance in other ways. These include:

- Lesson observations.

- Book scrutiny.

- Internal assessments.

- Moderation activities.

■ Discussions and interviews with pupils.

■ Hearing pupils read (and not just in primary schools).

In order to measure pupil performance, middle leaders must therefore have a strong presence in their colleagues' classrooms. They should regularly monitor teaching and learning in lessons, regularly undertake book scrutinies, and talk to pupils about their learning as often as possible. The evidence gathered in the classroom should be combined with careful data analysis of published performance data and with internal data sets, even though Ofsted inspectors no longer look at internal data during inspections.

47

How do I analyse data and pupil outcomes?

When teachers wonder whether they are ready to apply for middle leadership roles, it is often the thought of dealing with data that most concerns them, and it sometimes puts them off completely. Data analysis can be complicated and bewildering, but it doesn't need to be. Some colleagues genuinely enjoy burying themselves in data; they pore over dozens of different data sources and create dazzlingly complicated spread-sheets. Most middle leaders, however, look for a more straightforward route through the maze; they find what they need and move on. The key question with regard to data analysis at any level is, 'What do I want to know?' and the answer should be obvious: 'I want to know what went well and why; and what did not go well and why.' Effective leaders do not analyse data for purposes of self-aggrandisement, they do it to look for ways to improve outcomes for pupils.

It is not necessary to go into fantastic detail but a basic understanding of the data sources available, how to access them, and how they work is essential. Fortunately, most middle leaders are supplied with the data they need by the senior leadership team or, in secondary schools, by the data manager. There are some data sources, however, they need to seek out for themselves – examining board data, for example.

To begin with, care must be taken to distinguish between attainment data and progress data. Attainment data simply lists the grades or scores pupils achieve; progress data is much more sophisticated and allows an understanding of how well pupils perform compared to expectations and in context. Grammar schools like to publicise the high percentages of pupils achieving A* grades but, considering their attainment on entry, something would be wrong if they did not achieve such high grades. This may seem blindingly obvious, but it is a fact missed by so many advocates of grammar schools. On the other hand, a school may be regarded by parents as underperforming because so few pupils achieved A or A* grades, but in reality, it may have done a fantastic job in helping children who dramatically underachieved at Key Stage 2 towards a half decent set of GCSEs.

There are essentially four layers of data to consider:

1. National data sets.

2. Whole school data.

3. Subject level data.

4. Individual pupil data.

Middle leaders are most concerned with subject level data and individual pupil data, but they do need a basic understanding of national and whole school information. National data is published annually in a variety of forms. First comes the publication of the raw results – the scores and grades. Later performance tables are published which focus on key indicators and which allow comparisons to be made with other schools – the so-called league tables. Schools are provided with more detailed data sets in the form of the IDSR and ASP, both of which have restricted access, and many buy commercial packages which provide even more detail. These include systems such as SIMS and SISRA as well as more specific software packages which look at particular qualifications. ALPS (A-Level Performance System), for example, allows schools to measure the value they add to a pupil's A-Level performance compared to what might be expected of them following their previous academic performance at GCSE.

National data sets tend to focus on key indicators so their relevance to middle leaders varies according to the subjects for which they are responsible. The primary IDSR focuses on reading, writing and mathematics; the secondary IDSR on English, mathematics and the EBacc subjects. This means that leaders of non-core subjects in secondary schools and foundation subjects in primaries have to be very careful when exploring whole school data. Progress and attainment in foundation subjects is evaluated largely via internal data sets, though pupils' achievements in reading, writing and mathematics can be used to give colleagues a fair idea of their general levels of achievement across the board. Data on EBacc subjects is included in the secondary IDSR but care needs to the taken here. For example, while heads of science may find some useful information about their subject overall, if they want to explore progress in biology, chemistry and physics, they will need to look elsewhere. Similarly, the languages EBacc heading lumps all the languages taught in the school together, and humanities covers both geography and history. Geography may have performed spectacularly and history poorly but the two appear as one.

The ASP offers much greater detail, but it is not an easy system to navigate and its use is often restricted to senior leaders and data managers. It is accessed via the DfE website and it is password protected. It contains a wealth of information. For example, for each of the reading, writing and mathematics Key Stage 2 tests, it shows:

- The school's progress scores in reading, writing and maths.

- The percentage of pupils achieving the expected standard (a scaled score of 100 or more) in all of reading, writing and maths, compared to the national and local authority (LA) average.

- The percentage of pupils achieving the higher standard (a scaled score of 110 or more) in all of reading, writing and maths, compared to the national and LA average.

- The school's average scaled score in both reading and maths.

One can then delve deeper to:

- 'View pupil breakdown' – this offers a view of the graphs as scatter plots setting out the measure for each subject, for different groups.

- 'Explore data in detail' – this sets out the data out in table that provides a breakdown by pupil group and prior attainment. Filters can be selected in these tables to only show certain information, e.g. disadvantaged boys or girls in a low prior attainment band.

Similar information is available at secondary level covering English, mathematics, science, and the EBacc subjects. ASP does, however, provide information on individual subjects as well as relative performance indicators which can be very useful in considering the progress of one subject compared to others in the school. It also includes information on the numbers of entries per subject and this should not be overlooked. For example, a school website may boast about its fantastic results in French compared to other local schools but if they enter only 30 students out of a cohort of 150, they are bound to look good compared to schools where all pupils are entered.

Both ASP and the IDSR provide useful information covering the context of the school and the progress of groups. For example, leaders can access detailed whole school contextual information, including the percentage of the cohort who are:

- Girls.

- Ever 6 FSM (free school meals).

- Pupils with EAL (English as an additional language).

- Pupils with SEN support.

- Pupils with an Education, Health and Care (EHC) plan.

There is also information covering pupil ethnicity groups and it is possible to explore year group data for pupil groups and their prior attainment.

For senior leaders, ASP and the IDSR provides a wealth of additional information. The secondary IDSR, for example, includes headline information on:

- Overall Progress 8.

- Overall Attainment 8.

- Trends in subject entry or attainment.

- Data on behaviour, including exclusions.

- Attendance data.

- Destination data.

- Ethnicity.

- Pupil numbers.

- Disadvantaged and EAL pupils.

- SEND/SEN.

- Prior attainment.

It is useful for middle leaders to be aware of both whole school and national data, but they don't need to get caught up in the detail. They need to understand the context of the school, the educational background of the various cohorts, attendance and behaviour issues, and the percentages of various pupil groups, including SEND, disadvantaged, EAL etc. This allows them to consider the performance of their own subject areas in the context both of national and whole school performance.

So, how should middle leaders go about analysing subject specific data? In primary schools, subject leaders responsible for reading, writing and mathematics should begin by looking closely at the whole school data sets described above. Similarly, heads of English, mathematics and science in secondary schools should do the same. Those who lead EBacc subjects will garner some useful information from national data sets but, as we have seen, it will be fairly limited.

The starting point for all middle leaders is bound to be the raw data. All teachers await the publication of examination results with a mixture of excitement and dread. Most have a good idea what the results will look like, especially if robust moderation systems are in place, but there are always surprises. Experienced subject leaders know instantly if something has gone wrong and quickly begin to consider whether the issue is an internal one – something to do with the quality of teaching – or external, in which case an appeal to examining board needs to be considered. Middle leaders need to review results quickly and, as soon as data becomes available, look at the information provided by examining boards to see exactly how students have performed. In recent years, examining boards have facilitated much greater access to examination information. This includes question level data as well as the ability for schools to request pupils' scripts. Ironically, however, despite this degree of access, it is becoming steadily more difficult to appeal dubious results successfully.

By carefully analysing question level data, subject leaders can determine the questions candidates answered well and those where they struggled. This then allows teachers to look again at the curriculum and schemes of work and to make adjustments accordingly. Review of examination scripts is useful in enabling teachers to interpret mark schemes and to ensure that pupils are both well pre-pared and equipped with appropriate examination techniques.

When comparative data becomes available, subject leaders are in a position to compare the performance of their subjects both to others in the school and other nationally. As we have seen, this is not always straight forward. Heads of department often take great delight in crowing about their superb results without really considering their context. Primary schools enter all pupils for the Key Stage 2 tests, so comparisons are confined to the relative performance of pupils in reading, writing and mathematics. In secondary schools, however, relative performance is opaquer. The core subjects nowadays enter virtually all pupils, though there are some significant variations. While all pupils are likely to be entered for English Language, the numbers entered for Literature vary considerably (although the EBacc/Progress 8 stipulations have led to far more pupils being entered for both subjects nowadays). Maths generally enters everybody, but science is complicated by the choice of combined or separate sciences. General comparisons can be made between English and maths, or maths and science, but only up to a point. Nevertheless, a maths department where the results are significantly weaker than those in English will quickly come under scrutiny. Most heads of English, therefore, look first at their own data and then at maths.

For the EBacc and the optional subjects at GCSE, the picture is more complicated, and it is here that both numbers and context must be considered. Comparing attainment in French and PE, for example is fraught with difficulties. As we have seen, the French set could be small, and, let's be honest, languages tend to attract the brightest pupils whereas the PE cohort could be much larger and comprise a much wider range of abilities. Consequently, comparisons based on attainment are not particularly useful at all. Only when progress data is made available do such comparisons make sense. If the bright pupils who chose to do French did not get the grades they should have done, based on their prior attainment and their backgrounds, but the mixed ability pupils who chose PE did, then PE has clearly performed much better, despite having less dazzling attainment grades.

Most schools now have access to predictive data. For example, the use of Fischer Family Trust (FFT) data is now widespread. It uses sophisticated data analysis based on large national cohorts to make increasingly accurate estimates of pupil performance. In simple terms it estimates that this pupil, from this social class, with this prior attainment, born at this time of the year, with this gender and with this ethnic background, is likely, at this school, to achieve a grade in this range. Such estimates enable subject leaders to analyse pupil progress almost immediately examination results are released and thus come to a realistic appreciation of how well their subject has performed. Comparisons with other subjects are also possible and these will doubtless be scrutinised closely by senior leaders. When ASP is made available, relative performance can be looked at in even more detail.

Middle leaders will also want to look carefully at the progress of key groups of pupils: those with SEND, EAL etc. They should also consider gender and look closely at the progress of disadvantaged pupils in comparison to the whole cohort to see if initiatives aimed at closing the gap have been successful. Nor should the number of entries be ignored. The head of languages, for example, might well question why more pupils opt for Spanish as opposed to French; a head of humanities would do well to consider why more pupils choose geography than history. It is also important to consider progress over time. How has the subject performed over the last three years? Are standards rising? Is it becoming more popular, or are pupil numbers declining?

It is easy to spend too much time on data analysis to forget that data is only useful if one does something with it. Experienced heads of subject learn to dissect data sets quickly and to identify strengths and weaknesses. The identification of strengths allows pupils and colleagues to be congratulated and more of the same encouraged. The identification of weaknesses is more important, however, and should lead to deliberate steps to put things right. Analysis of data is all about improvement. The head of subject who looks at the data and sighs will be doing the same next year; the head of subject who makes changes is likely to see results improve year on year.

In order to analyse pupil outcomes successfully, middle leaders essentially have to work through a series of fairly obvious questions:

- What do the school's results look like overall?

- What is the school's context?

- What is attainment like in my subject?

- How much progress did pupils make in my subject?

- How did my subject perform compared to national outcomes?

- How does it compare to other subjects in the school?

- How did groups of pupils perform and is the gap closing?

- How did boys do in comparison with girls?

- How many pupils were entered?

- Has performance improved over the last three years?

- What does the question level data tell us?

Above all, what do we need to do to improve?

Of course, examination groups are not the only ones to be considered and similar questions need to be asked of internal data. By interrogating the performance of pupils at every stage of their journey through the school, constant improvement is possible. The key to a good set of Key Stage 2 results is good teaching at Key Stage 1 and in Reception; strong GCSE results depend upon good teaching in Year 7.

48

How do I ensure accurate predictions and assessments?

I once had a colleague who was convinced that he could accurately predict pupils' GCSE grades based solely on their names. He worked on the assumption that names were signifiers of class and social status and therefore the embodiment of some kind of self-fulfilling prophecy. Edwards and Katies were bound to get A grades; Waynes and Sharleens were doomed to get Ds and Es. The most worrying aspect of this theory, however, was that he was often right. Occasionally a Darren would achieve a good set of A grades but, on the whole, the list of top grades was dominated by traditional, middle class names. This was social determinism in action. A wild and undoubtedly uncomfortable theory certainly but it offers a salutary reminder of the difficulties inherent in making predictions.

Most schools, and most commercial software packages, now shy away from the term 'prediction' because it sounds too precise; instead, the term 'estimate' is used. An estimate allows some leeway so that potential outcomes are expressed in terms of a range of grades or scores. Instead of a firm prediction of a grade 5 at GCSE, a pupil will be given either a broader range, say 5–4, or a percentage chance of reaching a grade, for example: 15% grade 3, 60% grade 4, 25% grade 5. This recognises the difficulties of making accurate predictions and goes some way to acknowledging the range of factors at play in a pupil's education: social background, ethnicity, parental support, personal commitment, gender, age, enthusiasm for the subject, peer pressure, the quality of teaching, teachers' aspirations and so on. Despite the difficulties, however, teachers are expected to make predictions regarding pupil progress at every stage of their schooling and it is important that they do so. The predictions may not be particularly accurate, but they provide a mechanism for the measurement of progress.

Predictions are usually established using entry data. Whether it is children arriving at primary school from a nursery, or Year 7s starting secondary school, there is data available. The Foundation Stage Profile provides a baseline for pupils starting Year 1 and the Key Stage 2 tests a starting point for Year 7. This basic information is generally supplemented with other tests including Cognitive Ability Tests (CATs) and those that test reading and mathematical skills. Teachers know that such tests are not particularly accurate, and headteachers will always argue that the scores provided by previous providers are inflated, but they provide a framework on which to build.

Based on entry data, teachers can make predictions. A child who enters Year 7 with a test score of around 100, for example, should be aiming for a grade 4 or 5 at GCSE. Depending upon the school's assessment system, his or her progress towards this outcome can be measured each year to ensure that it is achieved. If the pupil falls behind, intervention can be put in place to get things back on track; if he or she outperforms predictions, then the predictions can be adjusted to offer greater challenge.

It took a while for the government to cotton on to the use of predictive data but eventually the concept of 'expected progress' was introduced, giving schools a more obvious set of targets to achieve. These were based on attainment not progress, and they did not take into account pupils' individual potential. So, at Key Stage 2 the expected standard in reading and mathematics was set at a scaled score of 100 or above. The expected standard in writing was described as a teacher assessment of 'working at the expected standard' (EXS) or 'working at greater depth within the expected standard' (GDS). The new expected standards were designed to be broadly similar but are not equivalent to the old National Curriculum level 4b. At GCSE, a C grade had long been regarded as a pass grade, though it was never expressed as such by the examining boards. Under the most recent system, there is still some confusion over the equivalent of a C grade, with both 4 and 5 competing for that honour. To clarify matters, the DfE eventually described a 4 as a pass and a 5 as a 'good' pass. The key point, however, is that teachers have national targets to aim for and these help to structure, and to some extent standardise, the predictions they make based on individual pupil data.

The use of FFT data is now widespread in schools across the UK and, as we have seen, it can be used to provide increasingly accurate estimates of pupil performance. It enables teachers to set targets for individual pupils based on national data sets which draw upon a huge amount of contextual information. These estimates are not, of course, 100% reliable but they add a certain amount of rigour to target setting. Teachers are thus able regularly to check whether an individual is working well and making progress in line with his or her estimates.

Schools should ensure that their teacher assessment judgements are moderated internally and, where possible, with other schools. This quality assures their judgements and provides a valuable opportunity for professional development. It is the job of the middle leader to monitor the assessment processes in class to ensure that teachers are aware of, and understand, each pupil's target grade, and are therefore able accurately to monitor each pupil's progress towards that grade. In primary settings, 25% of schools are subject to statutory external moderation by local authorities of a sample of their outcomes in reading, writing and mathematics. This validates judgements to ensure that they are consistent with national standards. It is a collaborative process between schools and local authority moderators.

Middle leaders are able to compare standards across each class via book scrutiny and lesson observations, but most introduce a series of standardised assessments. These can be conducted at the end of each unit of work or at the end of each year. The greater the frequency, the more comparable standards are likely to be, though care must be taken not to overburden colleagues with too many assessment points. As public tests and examinations draw near, much more material becomes available to support the moderation of standards. Teachers can draw on past papers, examination board exemplars and mark schemes, and the outcomes of mock examinations or practice questions.

Given the amount of material available, one would assume that teachers would therefore be able to make very accurate predictions. Unfortunately, this is far from the case. When pupils are entered for GCSEs and A-Levels, teachers have to submit predicted grades – these are particularly important at A-Level where university places are offered on the basis of these predictions – but they are surprisingly inaccurate. A study conducted jointly by the Institute for Education and the University and College Union in 2016 found that only 16% of applicants achieved the A-Level grade points they were predicted to achieve, based on their best three A-levels, with the vast majority over-predicted.[1]

The Corvid-19 crisis shone a bright light on predicted grades as teachers were suddenly forced dramatically to increase the accuracy of their predictions. Predicted grades replaced examination grades and the ultimate responsibility for pupil outcomes shifted away from the examination boards to schools. Of course, adjustments were made at every level: by teachers, middle leaders, senior leaders, examination boards and Ofqual, and, for the first time, final grades were based largely on teacher assessment rather than examination outcomes. There was inevitably a hue and cry about the accuracy of these results, but there has always been concern about the accuracy of examination results. It could be, however, that the system for awarding grades will change permanently as a result. It could be argued that the new pressure on teachers to make much more accurate assessments will lead to more accurate predictions; greater scrutiny will result in greater accuracy. If so, it may then be possible to place greater trust in teachers and thus give them much more prominence in the assessment process. We will have to wait and see.

Note

1 Wyness, G. 2016. *Predicted grades: accuracy and impact.* University and College Union. London. https://www.ucu.org.uk/media/8409/Predicted-grades-accuracy-and-impact-Dec-16/pdf/Predicted_grades_report_Dec2016.pdf

49

How do I measure impact in the classroom?

There is more to the measurement of impact than the analysis of data. It is important, therefore, for middle leaders regularly to consider the impact of the curriculum in the classroom. As we saw in the introduction to this section of the book, Ofsted inspectors certainly spend a considerable amount of time analysing pupil data to evaluate the impact of the curriculum in the classroom, but they also look closely at a range of other indicators. A wise middle leader will want to do the same.

The key to measuring impact in Ofsted terms is the phrase 'knowing more, remembering more and being able to do more.' A lesson visit should therefore involve asking questions which allow pupils to talk about what they know and what they can remember. Observations and time spent looking at pupils' books will provide evidence of what pupils are able to do.

A lesson observer should attempt to enter a lesson as unobtrusively as possible and yet ensure that pupils are aware that a visitor is present. In departments where collaboration is embedded in standard working practices this should be easy to do. Then, rather than diving into books or conversations with pupils straightaway, it is sensible simply to sit and watch what is going on. A huge amount can be learned in this way:

- Do pupils arrive on time?

- Do they look as if they are looking forward to the lesson?

- Do they get their books out quickly ready to begin?

- Does the teacher have a starter activity ready and do all pupils engage with it quickly?

- What is the atmosphere like?

- How strong/how warm is the relationship between the teacher and the class?

Within the first few minutes of a lesson it is possible to get a real sense of impact. If pupils arrive quickly, smile at the teacher and get straight down to their work, a positive climate for learning is in place. This suggests that learning is clearly likely to happen. The next consideration is the extent to which this initial impact is sustained:

- Are pupils able to concentrate for sustained periods of time?

- Does the teacher vary activities to maintain interest?

- Is there any low level disruption?

- Do pupils respond eagerly to questions?

- Is everyone involved in the lesson?

If pupils continue to concentrate and remain engaged with the lesson activities, the depth of learning increases and the impact is greater.

Once pupils are fully engaged in the lesson, an observer can begin to intervene more actively, albeit discreetly. Teachers should never be interrupted, and observers should do their best not to get in the way. Similarly, pupils should not be distracted for too long or taken away from their learning. A few general questions repeated with individuals around the class quickly provides additional information regarding impact:

- Are you enjoying the lesson?

- How does your teacher help you to learn?

- Is the work difficult?

- Do you feel challenged?

- Does the teacher make sure everyone understands things?

- Does the teacher listen to what you say in lessons?

- Do you find it easy to concentrate in this class?

- Do you feel comfortable asking questions when you don't understand something?

It is then important to delve a little deeper in order test pupils' understanding:

- Can you tell me what you have learned so far in this lesson?

- What did you do last lesson?

- Did you do anything last lesson which has helped you in this lesson?

- Is this lesson part of a unit of work?

- Can you remember what you were studying last week/last term?

- Have you encountered anything you didn't really understand?

- Did the teacher help you and do you understand it now?

- How well do you think you are doing in this subject?

- (For Years 5–6, 10–11 and the sixth form) How well do you think you will do in the exams?

- Do you have a target to aim for? Do you think you are on target?

- Do you get help from your friends?

- Do you sometimes find it hard to concentrate if others misbehave?

These are the questions which reveal what pupils know, what they can do and what they remember. Of course, don't expect pupils to remember everything, but those who are making good progress can usually talk enthusiastically about what they have learned and what they have done in previous lessons. In classes where the climate for learning is poor, pupils often struggle to remember things and tend to see lessons as discrete blocks of time with little connection between them. It is here that a poorly sequenced curriculum becomes evident. Units of learning which strike pupils as somewhat random are quickly forgotten; learning which is not returned to via recall in lessons, or interleaving, is unlikely to be remembered.

In primary schools, and in certain circumstances in secondary schools, observers should always listen to children read. This does not mean simply sitting there while a child reads out a page from a book; listening to a child read is a sophisticated activity. Begin with a series of simple questions:

- What book are you reading?

- Why did you choose it?

- Have you read it before? (A vital question for gauging fluency. A book that has been read many times will remembered and the reading will be automatic.)

- Is it a tricky book?

When the child begins to read, think about how fluently he or she is reading, how many words prove difficult, whether appropriate phonic techniques are applied to tackle tricky words, and whether the book is suitably challenging.

It is then important to check understanding. Some children are able to read fluently and convince adults that they are confident readers but, sometimes, fluency masks a lack of comprehension skills. So, ask about what has just been read:

- Tell me about the story.

- What happened before we started reading?

- What do you think will happen next?

■ Who is your favourite character?

and so on. By assessing the reading ability of a range of pupils in a class it is possible to gather evidence not only of the progress of individuals but about the impact of the reading curriculum, including the effectiveness of the phonics programme, the suitability of reading schemes, and the general reading culture.

The importance of looking at pupils' books has been discussed above (in the Implementation section) but it is worth noting here the value of talking to pupils about their books in lessons. The obvious checks can be made quickly as one walks around the class:

■ Do all pupils have their books with them?

■ Are they well presented?

■ Does the current page show that pupils take as much care with their work as they did at the start of the year?

■ Is there evidence of feedback?

■ Are errors and misconceptions corrected?

■ Is there evidence of effective curriculum sequencing?

■ Is there evidence of interleaving to help consolidate learning over time?

■ Is the standard of work appropriate to the age group?

The real impact of the curriculum can perhaps best be seen in the way pupils talk about their books. If they are proud of them and keen to show them to visitors (or in Years 10 and 11, where it is important for pupils not to look too keen, if they don't appear too reluctant to share them) it is easy to see that the subject has been enjoyed and taken seriously. Where the learning is strong, pupils can talk easily about what work they have done recently, how it relates to work done in class and how they have responded to the teacher's feedback. Again, a few simple questions will provide evidence of impact;

■ Tell me about your last piece of work.

■ What did you do to prepare for it?

■ How does it relate to earlier work in your book?

■ Has it taught you new skills or new knowledge?

■ Will your book help you to revise for tests and examinations?

■ Can you show me an example of an error you have corrected?

■ Can you show me where you have responded to your teacher's feedback?

Thus, skilled classroom observation allows middle leaders to evaluate the impact of the curriculum in considerable detail. The information gathered in lessons can then be compared to pupil data to give a fully rounded picture of pupil progress. Impact is not just about the data, it is about the climate for learning, the engagement of pupils in lessons, their ability to remember what they have learned, the quality of the work in their books, and their willingness to talk about what they have learned.

50

How do I evaluate impact on pupil groups – especially SEND and disadvantaged pupils?

When observing lessons and/or looking at books, it is always important to take note of the individual needs of pupils. In small schools, middle leaders will probably know the pupils in the classes they observe but in larger settings it is important to ensure that those with particular needs are easy to identify. Most teachers now have seating plans available which clearly identify individuals but if this is not the case, the observer will have to ask the teacher to point them out discreetly. It should then be possible to look closely at the work of individuals in the class without making it obvious that they have been selected for particular attention.

The focus of the observation should be the extent to which the curriculum meets the needs of every pupil. First, is the design of the curriculum sufficiently flexible so that it enables the teacher to make appropriate adaptations, if necessary, in order to meet the needs of all pupils and, second, is the teacher making the appropriate adaptations?

The mantra in many schools today is 'quality first teaching', meaning that the teaching is of sufficient quality to engage everyone in the class, and to a high level. Care must be taken here, however, as less committed colleagues could be tempted to assume that since they regard their teaching to be of a high quality, they therefore need to do nothing to support vulnerable pupils or to challenge the most able. Of course, good teaching does indeed reach all corners of the classroom, but it takes a great deal of thought to make sure it does so. Similarly, 'scaffolding' has now been replaced by 'scaffolding down', to suggest that teachers are preparing challenging lessons for which they then provide appropriate support to ensure that everyone rises to the challenge. If the process is carefully thought through, this can be a very effective pedagogical approach; if it simply means that teachers make all their lessons challenging without careful thought being given to individuals then it is likely to be much less successful.

The suitability of the curriculum for disadvantaged pupils and those with special needs can be gauged by the various activities described in the previous section on impact above. In other words, observers should do exactly the same things regardless of who is in the class: observe the lesson, talk to pupils, look at books etc. The main difference is that they are aware of individual needs and check to see that those needs are being met:

- Are all individuals engaged in the lesson? If not, is this because they don't understand the work, find it too difficult or are encountering barriers relating to their particular needs?

- Does the teacher regularly involve all pupils in class discussions and questioning sessions?

- Does the teacher tailor questioning to the needs of the pupil while retaining an appropriate level of challenge?

- Is the quality of the work in every pupil's book as good as that of their peers?

- Are there any gaps in the books and is there evidence that support has been given to help the gaps to be filled?

- Is there any evidence in their books of additional support if it is required? For example, if a pupil is withdrawn from a lesson to catch-up, is this noted and is the work they missed as a consequence of withdrawal from the lesson subsequently undertaken or supplied in note form?

- If there are teaching assistants in the room, how effectively are they supporting particular individuals? Are they supporting their learning or doing the work for them?

- What evidence is there of additional support beyond the classroom?

A subject leader should be well aware of the additional support offered to disadvantaged pupils and those with special needs, and this support should be monitored closely. If too much support is required, or is having minimal impact, then this may suggest that there is something wrong with the curriculum, or the way teachers are delivering the curriculum. The appropriateness and flexibility of the curriculum should therefore be kept under constant review.

Subject leaders should also regularly evaluate the impact of any additional support offered to pupils. Most schools offer lunchtime or after school catch-up sessions but there is little point in offering them if the pupils who need them don't attend. It is easy for middle leaders to assume that because such sessions exist, the support is in place, but the quality of support must be taken into account. Similarly, if pupils are withdrawn from lessons, do the benefits of being withdrawn outweigh the disadvantages of missing a lesson? And what about the quality of the additional support? One-to-one and small group sessions should be observed just as regularly as mainstream classes, and with the same rigour. An inspector may ask, for example, 'How confident are you that the small group sessions are of a high quality?' If one hasn't been seen in action, it will be difficult to answer, especially if the inspector has seen one already, which he or she is quite likely to have done.

Measuring the impact of the curriculum for disadvantaged pupils and those with special needs therefore extends well beyond the classroom.

Middle leaders should also have some input into the way pupil premium funding is spent and they should certainly be aware of how it impacts on the learning of disadvantaged pupils in their subject areas. If, for example, the fund has been used to supply a pupil with a laptop, it is important to consider whether the provision of a laptop has had a significant impact on his or her progress. If not, perhaps the money could be spent more effectively in ways more beneficial to the pupil's learning. At times, middle leaders may need to petition senior leaders for further funding if they have identified a curriculum adaptation which requires additional expenditure. The point here, of course, is that middle leaders need to look closely at all aspects of the support offered to disadvantaged pupils and those with special needs, including support beyond the classroom and the allocation of additional funding.

Disadvantaged pupils and those with special needs are quite rightly the subject of intense focus in schools and, indeed, during inspections. However, a similar approach as that outlined above should be taken with all pupil groups including looked after children, those with English as an additional language, those who are exceptionally talented etc. Awareness of pupil groups is not a question of categorisation but a way of ensuring that the curriculum meets the needs of all.

51

How do I provide evidence of impact for inspectors?

No matter how competent and well prepared a middle leader may be, an interview with an Ofsted inspector is a worrying prospect. With adequate preparation, however, it shouldn't be a particularly painful experience. Indeed, many now find they enjoy the challenge of a direct, stimulating conversation about pedagogy, and they find that they are proud to show off the work of their departments.

There are some obvious points to make about deep dive interviews:

- There is no need to be defensive. Inspectors will ask challenging questions, but they do so to gather evidence. There is nothing personal about their approach, and, though many teachers will find this hard to believe, most enter discussions with open minds.

- Be prepared. A leader who is able to provide examples, draw quickly on key sets of data, and talk knowledgably about what happens in his or her subject area inspires confidence. The more readily evidence is supplied, the shorter the interview and the more satisfied the inspector.

- Make sure what you say is happening really is happening. Too many middle leaders are able to talk confidently and fluently about the quality of teaching, monitoring systems, the quality of work in pupils' books, but if inspectors don't see these things when they visit lessons confident leadership becomes weak leadership.

- Take every opportunity to work with inspectors: visit lessons with them, look at books with them, and make suggestions regarding what would be good lessons to see.

- Don't overload them with paperwork. In a 45-minute interview, an inspector may be grateful for a sheet of A4 containing key pieces of information, but they are unlikely to be impressed with huge folders of policies and departmental procedures.

Effective middle leaders exude confidence. They are able to talk knowledgably about data, and they can respond easily to questions about pupil progress, and, in particular, the progress of particular groups. Although inspectors using the EIF are directed not to ask to see internal data, there is no reason why it shouldn't be discussed. A head of subject should be able to relate published data to current data to demonstrate sustained or improving performance. Thus, the data will evidence current and future impact.

Inspectors will ask, 'What will we see when we visit lessons?' and it is here that middle leaders have an opportunity to demonstrate both their leadership skills and a detailed knowledge of classroom practice. The conversation should be approached from the direction of the curriculum. In other words, what is the impact of the curriculum in the classroom? This allows leaders to talk about their vision for the subject, the structure and sequencing of the curriculum, how it is implemented in the classroom and how its impact is monitored. It may be useful to have evidence of lesson visits to hand, but much better evidence of the effectiveness of leaders in monitoring the work of the teachers and the progress of pupils in their departments is provided if inspectors see what they have been told they will see.

It is also important to be honest. A leader who insists that every teacher in the department is outstanding will lose all credibility when an inspector visits a lesson taught by a weak or inadequate teacher. Inspectors judge not only the quality of education but the quality of leadership. It is much better to point out that good teaching will be seen in these lessons but there is one teacher we have concerns about. Of course, in acknowledging weaknesses of any kind, it is important to be ready to explain what is being done to improve the situation. A head of subject who evaluates the quality of teaching and learning in his or her department accurately is much more likely to be regarded as a strong leader than one who paints an overly positive picture hoping to get away with it. Moreover, an inspector forewarned about a weaker teacher is very likely to view them in a more positive light, especially if evidence of support has been supplied. Remember that Ofsted judges the quality of education overall and not individual lessons.

As discussed above, evidence of impact will largely be drawn from lesson observations, book scrutiny and interviews with pupils. If middle leaders regularly visit lessons, they will know what inspectors are likely to see and will therefore have a good idea of the impact the curriculum is having on pupil progress. If they look at pupils' books regularly, they will be able to talk about the ways in which they show impact (evidence of curriculum sequencing and progression, useful feedback to which pupils have responded, high standards of presentation, very few gaps, evidence of support for pupils with particular needs etc.) And if they talk to pupils both in lessons and in small groups, they will be confident that individuals are able to talk about their learning with enthusiasm and understanding.

It is also important not to wait to be asked. A confident middle leader should point out the evidence inspectors need. For example, during a joint lesson visit, if the teacher is using questioning effectively, it might be appropriate to say to the inspector, 'We have worked extensively on improving questioning in the department, as you can see, and we think this is one of the reasons why our progress scores have improved this year.' Or, 'Here's an example in this book which shows clearly how the teacher has sequenced the topic and helped secure the pupil's understanding by ensuring that he has responded to feedback and thus learned more.'

Inspectors will generally appreciate having evidence pointed out to them – it makes their jobs much easier – but care must be taken not to be too directive. Inspectors are not averse to being gently nudged towards good practice in lessons, but they don't react well to overly prescriptive timetables. It may be that the subject leader is well organised and has arranged a series of lesson visits to make life easier for the inspector, but it is easy to give the impression that the visits have been arranged to avoid the less impressive parts of the school.

Most of the evidence inspectors need will be gathered during lesson visits and book scrutiny, but the importance of extra-curricular or co-curricular activities should not be overlooked. A clear account of the support activities run by the department gives a real sense that all pupils are catered for and a list of extra-curricular activities suggests that the department focuses on learning in its broadest sense – it is not all about examinations. The impact of such activities can be demonstrated both by attendance data and the way pupils talk about the activities they have been involved in when they are interviewed. Similarly, it is always useful to provide inspectors with evidence of progression: the number of pupils in a subject area who go on to study it at A-Level or at university, for example.

Providing evidence of impact for a good middle leader should therefore simply be a matter of explaining what they do. Good departments need do very little to prepare for an inspection if they are well led.

52

How do I handle the annual review with SLT and/or governors?

Almost as worrying as an inspection for many middle leaders is the annual department interview or review which most senior leaders now conduct. These usually take place in the autumn term following the summer's examination results and, in many cases, they involve a detailed discussion of the performance of the department across the course of the previous year. In primary schools the focus will, of course, be on the Foundation Stage Profile, phonics, and the Key Stage 2 tests, but pupil progress in all areas of the curriculum is likely to be discussed using internal data. In secondary schools, the initial focus will be on A-Level and GCSE results, but middle leaders should also be prepared to talk about the progress of pupils in every year group. Following the introduction of the EIF, subject review meetings are now beginning to spend time on the effectiveness of the curriculum as well as middle leaders' knowledge of the quality of teaching in their departments.

A well-prepared middle leader will have analysed subject specific data in detail and be able to talk confidently about overall progress, the progress of groups, and, if necessary, the progress of particular individuals. Senior leaders will have had access to most of the data, though they are unlikely to have looked at detailed examination board data, and they will have undoubtedly compared the performance of each subject area across the school. Middle leaders should therefore be able to discuss:

- The overall performance of their subject, both in terms of attainment and progress.

- The performance of groups.

- The performance of individuals, including both the high achievers and the under-achievers.

- Performance by teacher and class.

- Performance in comparison to national standards.

- Pupil numbers.

In addition, they should be prepared to outline:

- Any curriculum developments aimed at improving impact.

- Changing staff requirements.

- The quality of teaching in the department.

- The range of interventions undertaken.

Above all, they should be clear about the strengths and weaknesses of the department. Most annual reviews also include discussion of the school development plan and the department's response to it, and most schools now insist that departments create their own development plans. These should, of course, contribute to the whole school improvement agenda but also seek to improve identified areas of weakness.

This brings us on to the importance of self-evaluation. The annual subject review is, of course, an opportunity for senior managers and governors to interrogate middle leaders about the performance of their subjects, but it is also an opportunity for middle leaders to demonstrate the effectiveness of their self-evaluation skills.

The starting point, of course, is to know the strengths and weaknesses of each subject area. This will be based on the knowledge gained across the year via examination outcomes, internal assessments, lesson observations, book scrutiny, discussions with pupils and day to day contact with colleagues. It is important to be able to provide evidence and this should have been built up over the course of the year. It should include detailed analyses of examination and assessment data, records of lesson observations, notes from discussions etc. Senior leaders and inspectors will need to be convinced that middle leaders regularly monitor the quality of teaching. They won't want vague reassurance – 'I pop into their classes almost every day' – but an account of systematic observations and professional support.

Once issues have been identified, the next step is to map out in detail the steps taken, or planned to be taken, to bring about improvements. Headteachers like to be presented with solutions rather than problems. A head of department who can't explain why his or her results are so poor, or one who understands the problem but hasn't thought about how to put things right, is unlikely to inspire confidence. One who outlines clearly what the issues are and then details a series of carefully thought out actions to put things right is much more likely to be regarded as competent and professional.

As with inspectors, it is important not to be defensive. Celebrate success but admit the problems. Problems are usually obvious anyway, so there is really no point in trying to hide them or make them sound better. It is pointless trying to convince senior leaders that things are better than they really are; bluster and obfuscation is seen through easily. As a headteacher, I have sat through too many review meetings where heads of subject have sought to justify poor performance using every excuse available but without thinking for a moment about how to put things right.

Particularly memorable was a discussion with a head of department who assured me that his A-Level results were, in fact, much better than they appeared to be because, discounting the U grades, the rest of the class did really well.

The annual review should be regarded as a professional conversation. Very few senior leaders see it as a chance to appraise the performance of their middle leaders or catch them out; most see it as a chance to gain an overview of pupil performance across the school. Effective middle leaders use the annual review to martial evidence of performance, evaluate the work of their departments, and, above all, plan for improvement.

53

Finally, how do I know if I am doing a good job?

Self-evaluation is the key. Not just the evaluation of a particular subject or department but a review of personal progress. There will, of course, be formal opportunities for a curriculum leader's achievements to be measured – the performance management process, for example – but the most effective means is undoubtedly honest self-review. Middle leaders should be encouraged to take time out occasionally to sit down and think about how things are going and how effective they are in practice. The questions used to structure this book may be helpful, but the key areas can be summarised easily.

Intent:

▪ Do I have a clear vision for my subject and is this understood by my colleagues?

▪ How effective is my curriculum planning?

▪ Is the curriculum thoughtfully sequenced, does it cater for the needs of all pupils, and is it genuinely challenging?

Implementation:

▪ Is the quality of teaching in my subject of a high standard?

▪ Does teaching in my subject enable pupils to gain the knowledge they need to succeed?

▪ Are pupils learning more and remembering more?

▪ Do colleagues really take account of all pupils in their planning and teaching?

▪ Do they make every effort to close gaps?

▪ Do my colleagues really know what good teaching looks like?

▪ Are assessment practices strong? Do colleagues regularly check on pupils' learning?

- Do pupils make good use of teachers' feedback?

- How effective is staff development in my department?

Impact:

- Are examination outcomes strong and continuing to improve?

- Are assessments and predictions in my subject accurate?

- Is the positive impact of the curriculum obvious in lessons, in books and in conversations with pupils?

- Do pupils genuinely enjoy my subject?

- Is there a strong learning culture?

Above all, am I happy coming to work every day?

In schools with supportive headteachers, senior leaders and governors, there will be lots of opportunities for positive feedback. If a member of staff is doing a good job, the headteacher and line-manager should say so. However, only individuals themselves really know if they are doing well. The very best middle leaders know their strengths but remain on constant lookout for the chance to make improvements. Good teaching and strong leadership are never perfect but that doesn't mean one shouldn't strive for perfection.

Ultimately, good middle leaders have a clear understanding of the curriculum: they know what they intend it to do, they know how to implement it effectively, and they understand how to ensure that it has a powerful impact both on outcomes and pupil engagement.

Appendices

The appendix consists of a collection of examples and guidance documents. Illustrations from both the primary and secondary sectors are included. Maths and English have been used where specific subject content is needed but the examples can be adapted for any curriculum area.

Each example reflects current best practice, but they are by no means to be regarded as definitive. They are there to be used as a starting point for middle leaders to consider, discuss and, if necessary, disregard. They doubtless contain flaws and omissions, and some aspects will be subject to change over time, but as basic templates for further work they should be useful.

Appendix A
Example curriculum statement: primary reading

An introductory summary of the school's vision for the subject

Our vision is to foster a genuine passion for reading and we aim to ensure that all pupils become confident, enthusiastic readers. For children to develop strong reading skills, it is essential that they have a secure understanding of the letter sounds and spelling systems of the English language. We recognise that the precise acquisition of language helps create firm foundations. Phonics skills are developed through planned, systematic lessons which lead to fluency when blending and reading. Confidence with phonics provides the basis for the development of strong reading skills and to the enjoyment of a variety of books, the appreciation of different genres and the ability to access information independently.

A comment on the subject's importance

The ability to read underpins all areas of the curriculum. It equips children with the skills they need to understand and absorb knowledge from across the curriculum and, of course, it prepares them for life in the real world. The ability to read is absolutely essential and no child should leave school without the skills needed to navigate an increasingly sophisticated global landscape. Children will be taught to enjoy reading, to value and treasure books, and to learn skills which will stay with them throughout their lives.

A general outline of the subject as it grows and develops, an indication of how it builds upon what has gone before, and a brief outline of what happens in each Key Stage

From the moment children start school in EYFS, they are taught phonics. Children use and apply their knowledge and skills to read and write across the curriculum. Reading is practised daily through sharing stories, and their home reading books are closely matched to their phonic ability. We follow the Letters and Sounds programme which provides a structured and systematic approach to the teaching of phonics. It aims for children to develop fluent word reading skills and have good foundations in spelling by the end of Key Stage One.

High-quality phonics teaching secures the crucial skills of word recognition which, once mastered, enables children to read fluently and automatically. Once children are fluent readers, they are able to concentrate on the meaning of the text. Children need to acquire secure and automatic decoding skills and progress from 'learning to read' to 'reading to learn' – for purpose and pleasure. Regular monitoring allows staff to ensure that all children are making expected progress. All children are assessed half termly to ensure that if a child falls behind he or she can catch up quickly.

In Key Stages 1 and 2, children take part in daily reading sessions: all classes share a daily 'read aloud' session and children read their own books with increasing independence as they move up through the school. Children are heard reading regularly by teachers, teaching assistants and volunteers. All children are encouraged to read widely across both fiction and non-fiction to develop knowledge of themselves and the world in which they live. The understanding of vocabulary is key to the wider understanding of texts, so we celebrate the discovery of new words in our classrooms.

Key stage 1 reading books follow a system of coloured banding which is linked to the progression of phonic skills, ensuring that fluency is developed. When children progress to become free readers, they access a variety of books that have been chosen to encourage reading for pleasure.

Key stage 2 reading books are supported by the Accelerated Reader programme. Children are assessed at the end of Year 2 and then given a book level range from which to choose their books. This is then repeated termly throughout Key Stage 2. When a child has finished reading a book, they take a quiz which assesses their comprehension skills. In addition, we work hard to ensure that children encounter a wide variety of text types and we acknowledge that a great deal of the reading we all do today is on screen. We ensure, therefore, that children become familiar with all types of written texts including fiction, non-fiction, poetry, drama, web-based texts, letters, emails, etc.

Children are expected to read at home daily as this helps to develop confident and fluent readers. Children's reading logs are checked to ensure this is taking place and teachers have individual reward systems to support those who are active in their learning.

The department's approach to teaching

Staff constantly demonstrate and model the importance of reading. Children are taught through guided reading and they are given frequent opportunities to read independently. Accelerated Reader is used to support children's independent reading to ensure books are closely matched to their ability. Teachers employ a variety of methods in class including whole class teaching, individual support, drama activities, pair and group work. They also use a wide range of resources, including the latest ICT equipment.

The support provided for pupils of all abilities – SEND pupils, the most able etc.

We aim to ensure that every child's needs are catered for and every child is given the chance to become a competent reader. Teachers include all pupils fully in their daily phonics lessons. Through careful monitoring and tracking, teachers are able to identify children who may not be making expected progress and therefore need intervention to catch up with their peers quickly. Depending on the needs of individuals, this may include additional phonics teaching or support with decoding or comprehension skills. All children benefit from participating in and listening to other children demonstrating and explaining their ideas. Differentiated work, appropriate to individual children's needs, is provided in independent work during the day and also during intervention sessions. SEND pupils have specific literacy targets to be addressed during phonics lessons.

A brief indication of the extra-curricular activities aimed at enhancing pupils' experience of the subject

In order to support and enhance the teaching of reading, the school organises a wide range of extra-curricular activities. World Book Day is celebrated annually and visits from local authors are organised regularly. We have a wide range of library activities and staff are encouraged to share their reading with their classes. At the end of each term, Star Readers are chosen by staff and children receive certificates and prizes from the Head Teacher.

An indication of how pupils are prepared for what is to come – secondary schooling, university or the world of work

Class teachers work hard to prepare students for the next stages of their learning: from Reception to Key Stage 1, from Key Stage 1 to Key Stage 2, and from primary to secondary school. We work closely with our colleagues in the three local secondary schools to ensure that our reading curriculum prepares pupils for Year 7, and we all share the ambition to keep children reading throughout their lives.

A summary of the facilities available to the subject and a comment on how it is staffed

Reading is taught by every member of staff in every class. Our teachers are all equipped with the specialist skills they need to facilitate learning at every stage of a child's progress through the school. We are fortunate to have large, open classrooms, a well-stocked library, easy access to ICT facilities, and plenty of wall space to display children's work. We aim to ensure that there are books everywhere.

An indication of the department's success

Finally, our teachers are proud of the successes of their students. Key stage 2 Test results have been outstanding for the past three years, and well above national averages. More importantly, our children clearly enjoy reading and take great delight in sharing their reading with their teachers and their peers.

Appendix B
Example curriculum statement: secondary English

An introductory summary of the school's vision for the subject

The English department aims to provide an enriching and inspiring curriculum which encourages students to develop a lifelong appreciation of both the spoken and the written word. English enables students to develop strong communication skills, the ability to think critically, and a love of literature.

A comment on the subject's importance

The study of English underpins the study of all other subjects. It equips students with the skills they need to read, understand and absorb knowledge from across the curriculum. Whether it involves the rapid decoding of a question in maths, or the detailed analytical skills required in response to a topic in history, the ability to read with understanding is an essential skill. The texts students study, and the essays they write, stay with them throughout their lives and lead to a lifelong love of learning.

A general outline of the subject as it grows and develops, an indication of how it builds upon what has gone before, and a brief outline of what happens in each Key Stage

Students in Years 7 and 8 study a varied and engaging range of topics which build upon the skills gained in primary schools. All aspects of the National Curriculum are delivered through carefully designed units of work. Each unit includes formal assessments in reading and writing. Teaching consistently concentrates on accuracy in spelling, punctuation and grammar. However, the focus is always on enjoyment of the subject. Accuracy and imagination go hand in hand.

To develop English Language skills, students at Key Stage 3 learn to write for a wide range of audiences and different purposes, helping them to develop technical accuracy and fluency. Specific techniques are covered, including the analysis of the writer's craft and the evaluation of methods and techniques employed to bring the writing alive. Students are taught specific writing skills involving the use for effect of a wide variety of punctuation and sentence types, and they are encouraged to develop an increasingly sophisticated vocabulary. To inspire an appreciation of English literature, students read and analyse a range of texts including novels, poetry and plays from cultures around the world, as well as, of course, plays by Shakespeare.

All students at Key Stage 4 sit GCSEs in both English Language and English Literature. They study a range of Victorian writers, a modern novel and a Shakespeare play. In addition, they read and compare a range of non-fiction texts from the 19th, 20th and 21st centuries. Work on writing continues as students refine their skills to enable them to write for a variety of different audiences and purposes, with correct spelling, punctuation and grammar. The importance of creativity and imagination, however, cannot be underestimated and, despite the intense focus on examination preparation, enjoyment of the subject is always prioritised.

Following success at GCSE, students have the opportunity to continue studying English at A-Level. The department offers courses in both English Language and Literature, as well as being involved in the teaching of Drama and Media studies. The same approach to learning is taken in the sixth form with the focus remaining strongly on appreciation and enjoyment. Students of A-Level English learn to develop increasingly sophisticated analytical skills, read a wide range of texts, and hone their writing skills for further study. Full details are set out in the sixth form prospectus.

The department's approach to teaching

Classes in English are taught in mixed ability sets at Key Stage 3; students are set by ability at Key Stage 4 to maximise their chances of success in their GCSEs. Sets are carefully selected using both performance data and teachers' knowledge of individuals to ensure that every child is able to achieve his or her potential. The curriculum is designed to enable all students, whatever their individual needs, to make rapid progress. Teachers differentiate work to support students in class, but they are careful never to place a cap on learning potential. A variety of methods is employed to make teaching both effective and engaging. These include pair and group work, the use of a wide range of interactive resources, drama, debate, questioning, and individual support. Success arises from a desire to achieve combined with a positive work ethic. Consistent effort as well as high attainment is always celebrated.

The support provided for pupils of all abilities – SEND pupils, the most able etc.

Staff work hard to ensure that pupils of all abilities are encouraged to do well. Teachers work closely with the special needs department to provide appropriate support in every lesson and the work of every student is monitored closely.

Where extra help is needed, a variety of additional support is provided: this includes Year 7 catch-up sessions, lunchtime revision classes, small group activities led by specialist teachers and individual mentoring. The English department is fortunate in having access to a range of specialist provision to support students with special needs or disabilities, those whose first language is not English, disadvantaged pupils and those with behavioural issues. There is also an exciting programme of activities to challenge and inspire all students to take their learning well beyond the curriculum.

A brief indication of the extra-curricular activities aimed at enhancing pupils' experience of the subject

In order to support and enhance the teaching of English, the department organises a wide range of extra-curricular activities. Students regularly visit both local and national theatres, and there are strong links with both The National Theatre and The Royal Shakespeare Company. Every summer the school runs a writer in residence programme which gives students the chance to work with professional writers. The department also publishes a regular student creative writing magazine and works closely with the library to ensure that the books on offer are stimulating and up to date.

An indication of how pupils are prepared for what is to come – secondary schooling, university or the world of work

English teachers work hard to prepare students for the next stages of their learning: from Key Stage 3 to Key Stage 4, from GCSE to A-Level, from A-Level to university, and from A-Level to the world of work. As well as ensuring they leave school with the essential skills needed to secure worthwhile employment, teachers work closely with students to support them when applying for sixth form colleges and universities.

A summary of the facilities available to the subject and a comment on how it is staffed

There are eight full time and two part-time English teachers, all of whom are subject specialists. The English department is well equipped, with eight classrooms based around a central open learning area and easy access to a dedicated ICT suite. At the heart of the school is a well-stocked library and each classroom has its own class library. English teachers regularly use the drama studio and the hall stage to enliven their lessons and to bring drama texts to life.

An indication of the department's success

Finally, English teachers are proud of the successes of their students. GCSE English results have been outstanding for the past three years, and well above national averages. A-Level English attracts large numbers of students, many of whom go on to study English at university

Appendix C
Example curriculum plan:
Y6 Maths

	Autumn 1	Autumn 2	Spring 1	Spring 2	Summer 1	Summer 2
Topic	Numbers and problem solving	Fractions and geometry	Decimals, percentages and algebra	Measurement and ratio	Geometry and statistics	Investigations and preparation for KS3
Learning objectives	To develop fluency in place value and number calculations including addition, subtraction, multiplication and division.	To develop confidence in using fractions, progressing from number lines to multiplication and division. To explore position and direction in geometry.	To develop fluent use of decimals and percentages, using real-life examples. Use algebra to solve two step equations.	To calculate and convert units of measurement. Recognise when it is possible to use formulae for area and volume of shapes.	Understand shapes based on their properties and sizes. Find unknown angles in any triangles, quadrilaterals and polygons. Develop basic statistical skills.	To consolidate skills and knowledge acquired in years 5 and 6 in order to prepare for Year 7.
Knowledge/ skills to be gained	Core number skills. Problem solving skills.	Fractions: adding, subtracting, multiplying, dividing. Equivalences: decimals and percentages. Geometry: coordinates, translation and reflection.	Decimals: multiplication and division, fractions to decimals. Recall and use equivalences between simple fractions, decimals and percentages. Basic algebraic skills.	Confidence with measurement. Familiarity with shape, area, perimeter and volume. Problem solving skills using ratio.	Calculation of angles, shape drawing, understanding of nets. Draw and interpret line graphs and pie charts.	Investigative skills. Mastery skills.

(Continued)

	Autumn 1	Autumn 2	Spring 1	Spring 2	Summer 1	Summer 2
Assessment	Teachers check on learning in every lesson. Compare current progress with Y5.	Summative assessment based on number and fractions.	Teachers check on learning in every lesson. Formative percentage and algebra assessment.	Practice test papers.	KS2 Tests.	Learning gaps identified via consolidation exercises.
Links with prior/ subsequent learning	Build upon and consolidate Y5 maths knowledge and understanding.	Y5 knowledge of fractions, decimals.	Link knowledge of fractions and decimals to percentages.	Consolidation of prior knowledge of measurement, shape etc.	Revision of key skills covered in Years 5 and 6 required for KS2 tests.	Outline key topics to be explored in Y7 and show how they will build upon work done this year.
Literacy/ numeracy skills	Key vocabulary: *Compare, round, negative, common factors, common multiples, prime squared, cubed, operations, estimations.* Focus on real world numeracy.	Key vocabulary: *fraction, compare, order, denominator, integers, whole, quadrant, translation, reflection.*	Key vocabulary: *integers, percentage, increase, equivalence, algebraic, equation, enumerate* Explore the language of assessment for the KS2 tests.	Key vocabulary: *metric, imperial, parallelogram, cuboid, volume ratio, scale, proportion.* Practice writing skills for tests.	Literacy and numeracy skills required for the tests.	Revision of key mathematical terminology.

Appendix D
Example curriculum plan: Y7 Maths

	Autumn 1	Autumn 2	Spring 1	Spring 2	Summer 1	Summer 2
Topic	From number to algebra	From number to statistics	Geometry and ratios	Proportion and probability	From algebra to geometry	From number to geometry
Learning objectives	To build upon Y6 learning and to develop fluency in place value and number calculations. To explore algebraic notation in further detail.	To consolidate and build upon KS2 number knowledge – complex fractions and decimals. To introduce more complex statistical diagrams and averages.	To explore geometry including angles and properties in a wide range of shapes. To familiarise pupils with increasingly complex uses ratio using real-life examples.	Building upon ratio, to introduce proportion using real-life examples. To introduce the concept of probability.	To develop links between algebra and geometry. To apply transforma- tions.	To introduce the geometry of shapes including their properties. To develop greater fluency in calculation, including complex negative numbers.
Knowledge/ skills to be gained	Core number skills. Algebra skills.	Improved calculation skills involving decimals and fractions. Key principles of statistical analysis.	Knowledge of angles, drawing and measuring.	An understan- ding of the applications of propor- tion, including conversion. An unders- tanding of probability.	The application of sequences and their application to linear graphs. The ability to explore transforma- tions and apply them to a coordinate grid.	A detailed understan- ding of shape, area and perimeter. The ability to calculate using different methods, including negative numbers.
Assessment	Teachers check on learning in every lesson. Baseline assessment/ KS2 comparison.	Summative assessment based on number algebra and statistics.	Teachers check on learning in every lesson. Formative geometry assessment.	Summative assessment drawing together geometry, ratio and probability.	Teachers check on learning in every lesson.	End of year summative assessment. Learning gaps identified.

(Continued)

	Autumn 1	Autumn 2	Spring 1	Spring 2	Summer 1	Summer 2
Links with prior/ subsequent learning	Build upon Y6 maths knowledge – e.g. negative numbers, prime numbers, order of operations etc.	KS2 knowledge of fractions and decimals.	Build upon pupils' knowledge of shapes and angles.	Build upon work on ratio.	Build upon KS2 work on graphs and use of co-ordinates.	Outline key topics to be explored in Y8 and show how they will build upon work done this year.
Literacy/ numeracy skills	Develop familiarity with new mathematical language. Set out guidance for completing work in books.	Understand statistical terminology. Explore the language of assessment in maths.	Ratio terminology. Language of geometry.	The language of probability. Check the quality of presentation in exercise books, including grammar and spelling.	Revision of key mathematical language from previous topics.	End of year exercise book review. Compare first and last pages. Compare, if possible, with Y6 work-books. Create list of key mathe-matical words.

Appendix E
Guidance: marking and feedback

Marking and feedback policies vary from school to school. Middle leaders should work within whole school policies but shape them to ensure that they meet the needs of pupils in their particular subject areas. What follows is essentially a summary of good practice which can be used as a starting point to develop specific subject guidance. Guidance for subject teachers should be kept simple, agreed by all, and monitored closely to ensure that it is implemented consistently across the department or subject area. Pupils should understand the guidance, recognise that it is used regularly, and know how to respond to feedback.

Key Principles

- Teachers do not simply mark books; they provide feedback to help pupils learn

- The sole focus of feedback is to advance pupils' learning

- Feedback varies by age group, subject and what works best for the pupil and teacher

- Teachers use information from feedback to identify pupils' common difficulties and to plan appropriate learning experiences for individuals/groups/classes

- The quantity of feedback should not be confused with quality. The quality of the feedback, however given, will be seen in how well pupils tackle subsequent work

- Feedback can take a variety of forms: teacher to student; student to teacher; student to student; written and verbal; focused on classwork, homework and assessments

- Teachers' workload should be manageable. There is very little evidence to support the current widespread practice of extensive written comments. Instead, teachers should focus on enabling pupils to learn from their mistakes, or extend their learning, rather than covering the page with obvious evidence of 'traditional' marking

- Parents need to be kept informed to help them understand how their children's work will be marked and how it will help them to learn

- Subject feedback practices operate within the whole school policy.

Effective feedback should:

- acknowledge and value pupils' efforts and achievements

- prompt a response from the student

- be specific, accurate and clear

- encourage and support further effort

- be given sparingly so that it is meaningful

- identify the 'learning gaps' of individual students

- put the onus on students to correct their own mistakes, rather than providing correct answers for them

- encourage pupils to discuss and reflect upon their own work

- monitor progress in knowledge, understanding and application

- alert the teacher to misconceptions, so that the teacher can address these in subsequent lessons.

Literacy

Every teacher is a teacher of literacy. When marking for literacy, all staff should use the whole school marking code. The code forms an integral part of the literacy policy and should be displayed in every classroom.

SP	Spelling to correct
P	Punctuation to correct
//	New Paragraph needed
g	Grammar to correct
S?	Not a sentence
^	Missing word
W	Wrong word
P	Good point made
PP	Very good point made
?	Unclear/What does this mean?

Methods

- Teachers comments should be brief, legible and intelligible to pupils

- Comments should identify both positives and next steps so that pupils have a clear understanding of how to move their learning forward

- Personalised verbal feedback is the most frequent form of feedback and should be embedded within every session. It is designed to enable students to make immediate improvements to their work

- Verbal feedback may well be directed to individuals or groups of students. Teachers may wish to record verbal feedback with their initials or FB, but the most effective verbal feedback will be evidenced by an improvement in a pupil's work

- Pupils may mark their own work or that of others when and where appropriate under clear teacher guidance

- Feedback sheets or checklists may be used where appropriate

- Stamps, stars and stickers may be used where appropriate, but not overused

- Good work should be celebrated whenever possible

- Spelling errors should be corrected. Not all errors will be corrected, however. There will be a focus on high frequency words, common mistakes and subject-related words

- High standards of presentation should be encouraged at all times.

Ofsted and Feedback

- Ofsted does not specify the frequency, type or volume of marking and feedback

- Teachers and leaders use assessment well, for example to help pupils embed and use knowledge fluently, or to check understanding and inform teaching. Leaders understand the limitations of assessment and do not use it in a way that creates unnecessary burdens on staff or pupils.

Appendix F
Guidance: knowledge organisers

Dozens of knowledge organisers are available on the internet. The variety is really quite bewildering, and virtually all aspects of the curriculum are covered including key learning skills, individual subject plans, and specific guides to individual texts. Commercial packages are readily available, most of which are tied either to the National Curriculum or specific examination syllabuses. However, the best ones are designed in-house to ensure a direct link with the curriculum as it is delivered on a day to day basis in lessons.

Knowledge organiser templates are also readily available but for those who plan to design their own, many of the features included in effective organisers are listed below. The recommended approach is to be selective: choose only those headings that apply, and don't choose too many.

Knowledge organisers headings *(tick those that are appropriate)*

- Key vocabulary ☐
- Key places and people ☐
- Key dates (e.g. in history) ☐
- Equations and formulae ☐
- Explanatory diagrams to aid memory ☐
- Key themes ☐
- Key characters (for English literature) ☐
- Key questions ☐
- Key concepts ☐
- Significant quotations ☐

- Model sentences ☐
- Essay structure guidance ☐
- Simple timelines ☐
- Health and safety notes (for science and DT) ☐
- Useful website links ☐

Appendix G
Guidance: department self-evaluation

Part 1 – Examination Analysis

Learning/development plan

Write a brief summary of your Department's progress against each of your targets from last year's Learning Plan.

1.

2.

3.

Key issues arising from examination performance:

Identify the key issues evident from a detailed analysis of examination performance - e.g. lack of top grades, underperformance of boys, concerns over coursework, etc.

1.

2.

3. etc.

Progress:

Analyse the progress made by students in your subject, commenting specifically on the progress of Disadvantaged (Pupil Premium) students

1. Progress overall:

2. Pupil Premium:

3. SEND:

Key successes and strategies to build on those successes:

1.

2.

3. *etc. if necessary*

Part 2 – General Self-evaluation

Write a brief summary of your department's overall performance using the following questions:

1. How good is student attainment in your department?

   This section should include a detailed class by class analysis of your headline examination results compared to previous years and where possible national results sets. Identify any issues arising (e.g. underperformance off boys, or lack of top grades etc.) and any action points. Make specific reference to the achievement of particular groups within your subject area (e.g. Disadvantaged/PP students SEND, students with high, middle or low PA (prior attainment), boys/girls etc.)

2. How good is student progress in your department?

   This section should include a detailed class by class analysis of your examination results. You need to show how pupils have progressed from R to KS1, KS1 to KS2, KS2 to KS4, and from KS4 to A-Level. Is pupil progress in line with targets? Make specific reference to the achievement of particular groups within your subject area (e.g. Disadvantaged/PP students SEND, students with high, middle or low PA (prior attainment), boys/girls etc.)

3. How effective is your subject curriculum?

   How have you organised (sequenced) your curriculum? How do you plan for progression (from early years to end of Key Stage 2, or from Year 7 to Year 11/13)? What changes do you plan to make in the light of your evaluation of the success of the curriculum last year?

4. How effective is learning in lessons in your department?

   This section should include reference to the data above as well to your records of lesson monitoring. You must make it clear how you monitor learning in your department.

5. How effective is assessment in your department?

   Give clear examples of how you ensure that progress in years and between teachers is tracked, identifying areas for development. You may wish to use the outcomes of any recent review. Focus particularly on how assessment is used to inform progress.

6. What are your CPD requirements for this year?

   Outline the strengths and weaknesses of teaching in your subject and your plans/requests for training to improve matters.

Appendix H
Guidance: line management

Purpose

- To build successful departments and outstanding leadership

- To monitor student progress in subjects and in year groups

- To identify approaches to address underperformance

- To revisit and assess the extent planned actions in classrooms are improving student progress

- To develop consistent approaches to key teaching priorities

- To share best practice

- To discuss management issues and agree next steps

- To share the challenges of leadership and offer help

Frequency

- 1 hour per fortnight

- With newly appointed subject or year leaders – meetings may be jointly held so best practice is modelled

Audience for minutes

Written by the line manager for (in order of priority):

- Subject leader

- Team

- Line manager

- Head teacher

Typical headings used for discussion:

1. Progress and standards

2. Progress of disadvantaged groups

3. Curriculum developments

4. Development of teaching and learning

5. Lesson drop-ins

6. Leadership of the team

7. Management – weekly/day to day issues

8. AOB

Line Management Meeting Template

Subject: _____ **Staff:** _____&_____ **Date:**

Progress and standards	
Intervention – vulnerable and disadvantaged students	
Day to day management	

CPD/ Developing teaching and learning in team	
Curriculum/ assessment developments	
AOB	

Appendix I
Guidance: how to prepare for a deep dive

The Ofsted framework is based around deep dives. These are essentially detailed investigations of particular subjects and they will nearly always cover at least one of the core subjects. Reading is always subject to a deep dive in primary schools; maths and English are not compulsory, but they are nearly always chosen. In addition to the core subjects, any other subject can be chosen, and, in most schools, inspectors look at four or five areas. Middle leaders therefore need to be ready. Of course, preparation for a deep dive is also preparation for good middle leadership.

Inspectors arrive in school having had a good look at the published data and the information on the school website. The lead inspector will have discussed the strengths and weaknesses of each academic subject and will have agreed the deep dives. It is important, therefore, for middle leaders to talk to the head about that initial discussion.

On the day, inspectors will want to meet the curriculum lead for the subject they plan to investigate first thing – if possible. The day will look something like this:

1. **A forty-minute discussion** of the curriculum and the subject department. The main areas discussed include:

   a.   The curriculum offer

   b.   Subject planning and sequencing

   c.   Pedagogy

   d.   Teachers' subject knowledge

   e.   Ambition for all

   f.   Disadvantaged pupils

   g.   SEND pupils and other groups

2. **Lesson visits**. Subject leaders or senior leaders will be offered the chance to accompany inspectors to visit a selection of lessons. Inspectors will choose the lessons, but they can be gently steered if necessary. They will want to see at least two year groups (although in primary schools they generally have time to visit most year groups) and they will spend only about fifteen or twenty minutes in each lesson. The aim is to judge the quality of education, not the quality of teaching in each lesson. Leaders will be expected to discuss what they have seen with the inspectors (this adds to the leadership judgement), but this should be seen as an opportunity to provide a more rounded picture of the learning seen. Inspectors will talk to students, and they will focus in particular on pupil groups. They will also look at pupils' books and discuss their work with them.

3. **Book scrutiny**. This can take place at any time of the day and it is useful for the subject leader to be present. Inspectors will ask to see a full range of books from at least two year groups and they may indeed select them themselves. They are most likely to choose books from the classes they have visited earlier in the day.

4. **Meetings with pupils** take place throughout the inspection. Deep dives normally involve a meeting with pupils drawn from two year groups but inspectors could ask to see particular groups – e.g. pupil premium students, or those with SEND. Pupils will be asked to bring their books along so they can talk about them. These meetings usually involve unaccompanied inspectors.

5. **Meetings with staff**. At the end of the day, inspectors may ask to meet members of a subject department, usually without the presence of the subject leader. This is essentially a check on attitudes, collaboration, climate for learning, consistency and workload.

6. Inspectors will offer feedback to middle leaders during the course of the day, but they are unlikely to feedback to individual teachers unless they are asked to do so. It will be up to middle leaders to feedback to their colleagues.

7. At the end of day one and at the end of the inspection, inspectors share their findings with their colleagues, observed by the head and one other member of the leadership team, to help them judge the quality of education overall.

In lesson visits, discussions with pupils and work scrutiny, these are the questions inspectors are likely to ask:

- What are pupils (including disadvantaged and those with SEND) learning?

- What do pupils know, understand and are able to do?

- What can pupils remember about previous work on this topic?

- How well are pupils able to use, apply, transfer and generalise what they have been learning? How independent are pupils at this?

▦ How well are pupils, particularly those with SEND, supported?

▦ How close is the correlation between the EHCP/SEN support plan and the work and classroom arrangements?

▦ What do connected examples of pupils' work show about how well pupils are building up their knowledge, understanding and skills?

▦ What are pupils' hopes for their future?

▦ How is what pupils are learning preparing them to realise their hopes?

▦ How do teaching staff assess pupils' learning? How effectively is this information used to adapt learning and make choices about how best to support pupils?

Appendix J
Guidance: deep dive questions

Subject-specific questions

■ Please outline the context of your subject within the school. How do whole-school priorities affect your subject?

■ What do you want pupils to know, understand and be able to do by the end of the term/year/Key Stage?

■ Why do you teach what you teach (selection)?

■ How have you organised (sequenced) your curriculum?

■ How do you plan for progression (from early years to end of Key Stage 2, or from Year 7 to Year 11/13)?

■ How does the content taught in previous years/topics/lessons prepare pupils for what they are about to learn?

■ How do your plans ensure that they meet the needs of pupils with SEND and disadvantaged pupils? How will this be seen in class?

■ Is there any liaison with the previous/next Key Stage in other school(s)?

■ How is assessment used in your subject? Does it check that necessary components are learned before attempting composite tasks?

■ What extra-curricular activities do you offer in your department and what do you do to widen participation?

■ What training have you had in subject knowledge and subject-specific pedagogy?

■ What training have your colleagues had in subject knowledge and subject-specific pedagogy? What arrangements are in place for NQTs, inexperienced and non-specialist and struggling teachers?

■ What do you expect to see in the lesson visits today?

General wider questions

- What is it like to work in this school? Does it have a distinctive culture?

- What are the expectations for pupils' behaviour?

- How do systems ensure that low-level disruption is dealt with effectively?

- How does the school respond to bullying?

- How does the school develop pupils' spiritual, moral, social and cultural development? How are the most disadvantaged provided for?

- Do leaders ensuring that you have a reasonable work-life balance? Have you experienced any harassment or bullying?

- What safeguarding training have you received? What have you done differently as a result?

Appendix K
Guidance: work scrutiny

- Is teaching focusing on the correct **skills and subject content** for pupils' age/stage?

- Do the books show well-**sequenced** work?

- Are pupils able to **recall** prior learning in later tasks?

- How effective is the use of **assessment**? Are misconceptions corrected quickly? Do pupils learn from their mistakes?

- Is there evidence that pupils are putting appropriate effort into their work? Is work presented well and completed? Does the work reflect good or better **attitudes** to learning?

- Are lower-attaining pupils **catching up** quickly enough? Where they have not grasped concepts or secured skills, is there evidence of additional work to help them to consolidate their understanding?

- Are pupils with **special educational needs and/or disabilities** receiving work that enables them to make strong progress? Are ambitions and expectations high enough?

- Are **disadvantaged** pupils receiving work that enables them to make strong progress? Are ambitions and expectations high enough?

- Does the work reflect that teachers have high **expectations** of all pupils? Is this reflected in their feedback to pupils, their attention to detail and the demands they make of pupils?

- Does work reflect that, over time, pupils are making **good gains in knowledge**, understanding and skills and, where appropriate, catching up quickly to expected levels of attainment for their age?

- Does the quality of teaching seen in books reflect the impact of **leaders'** work to improve the quality of education?

- Does the quality of education seen indicate that leaders' **self-evaluation** of the quality of education is accurate?